Group Psychotherapy and Managed Mental Health Care

A Clinical Guide for Providers

Mental Health Practice Under Managed Care
A Brunner/Mazel Book Series

S. Richard Sauber, Ph.D., Series Editor

> The Brunner/Mazel Mental Health Practice Under Managed Care Series addresses the major developments and changes resulting from the introduction of managed care. Volumes in the series will enable mental health professionals to provide effective therapy to their patients while conducting and maintaining a successful practice.

3. Solution-Oriented Brief Therapy of Adjustment Disorders: A Guide for Providers Under Managed Care
   By Daniel L. Araoz, Ed.D., and Marie A. Carrese, Ph.D.

2. Group Psychotherapy and Managed Mental Health Care: A Clinical Guide for Providers
   By Henry I. Spitz, M.D.

1. Psychopharmacology and Psychotherapy: Strategies for Maximizing Treatment Outcomes
   By Len Sperry, M.D., Ph.D.

Mental Health Practice Under Managed Care, Volume 2

Group Psychotherapy and Managed Mental Health Care

A Clinical Guide for Providers

Henry I. Spitz, M.D.

Brunner/Mazel *Publishers* • New York

Library of Congress Cataloging-in-Publication Data

Spitz, Henry I.
  Group psychotherapy and managed mental health care: a clinical guide for
  providers / Henry I. Spitz.
      p.   cm. — (Mental health practice under managed care ; v. 2)
  Includes bibliographical references and indexes.
  ISBN 0-87630-791-8 (pbk.)
  1. Group psychotherapy. 2. Managed mental health care.
  I. Title. II. Series: Mental health practice under managed care ;
  2.
    [DNLM: 1. Psychotherapy, Group—organization & administration.
  2. Psychotherapy, Brief—organization & administration. 3. Managed
  Care Programs—organization & administration.   WM 430 S761g 1995]
  RC488.S646 1995
  616.89'152—dc20
  DNLM/DLC
  for Library of Congress   95-36970
                                                                             CIP

Published by
BRUNNER/MAZEL, INC.
19 Union Square West
New York, New York 10003

Manufactured in the United States of America

10   9   8   7   6   5   4   3   2   1

To Susan, Becky, and Jake,
my constant sources of love and inspiration.

Contents

Preface   ix

PART I: INTRODUCTION TO MANAGED CARE AND THE BRIEF
          GROUP THERAPIES

  1.   *General Principles of Managed Mental Health Care in the*
       Clinical Setting   3
  2.   *Brief Group Psychotherapy: Historical Perspectives and*
       Contemporary Trends   16
  3.   *Overview of the Pragmatics of Brief Group Therapy in the*
       Context of Managed Mental Health Care   29

PART II: CLINICAL ISSUES IN MANAGED CARE GROUPS

  4.   *Practical Concerns for Leaders of Managed Care Groups*   45
  5.   *Construction of the Managed Care Group*   58
  6.   *Preparation of Prospective Group Members for Group Entry*   69
  7.   *Stages of Group Development and Their Significance in the*
       Managed Care Setting   86
  8.   *Conduct of the Initial Stage of Managed Care*   97
  9.   *The Middle Stage of Brief Groups: Problems and Solutions*   113
  10. *Termination of the Group and Follow-up Planning*   127

PART III: SPECIAL ISSUES

   11.   *The Inpatient Group and Groups with Unique Patient
       Populations*   139

PART IV: DOCUMENTING THE GROUP EXPERIENCE AND
              EVALUATING THE OUTCOME

   12.   *Recording and Reporting the Managed Care Group Experience*   159
   13.   *Evaluating the Outcome in Brief Group Psychotherapy*   170
   14.   *Future Directions and New Challenges*   176

   Appendix A: *American Group Psychotherapy Association, Inc.
                      Guidelines for Ethics*   185

   Appendix B: *National Registry of Certified Group Psychotherapists
                      Instruction Guidelines for Completing
                      Eligibility Form*   189

   References   195

   Name Index   201

   Subject Index   203

Preface

The changes in health care that have been slowly evolving over recent years have ignited and caused a major upheaval in the entire system, leaving confusion, hope, and despair in their wake. Mental health care and substance abuse services face an uncertain future which has left many in these fields with a sense of grave concern regarding what the future holds.

The ways in which mental health care services will be redesigned, delivered, and paid for are all currently up for review. Only one thing seems certain—our present system of health care management is too costly to continue in its current form and change will continue.

In response to this trend, nearly everyone with a vested interest in mental health care has responded by creating a variety of proposed plans or solutions for this agonizing dilemma. The changes in mental health care financing alone have made many proposals obsolete or irrelevant even at this early stage of the game. The debate surrounding the governmental health care reform plans is the tip of an iceberg that has at its base many more alternative plans, conflicts of interest, issues of advocacy for different causes, and a host of moral and ethical issues that all require careful study and examination.

The impetus for this text are the changes that health care reform has already produced by its impact on the level of the clinical practice of mental health service delivery. Managed care is here and, whether or not it is here to stay, it is a complex, nonunified system that directly affects the basic foundation of the mental health care tradition: the relationship between the patient and the therapist.

Clinicians, now called providers, are mobilized in both constructive and questionable ways. Many are accepting the changes and are trying to create ways of working within the current system in a manner that allows them to maintain their professional and economic integrity. Others are vehemently opposed to managed mental health care in any form and are either trying to propose realistic alternatives or "bucking the system" in a variety of ways.

This book is addressed to a segment of the population embroiled in the managed mental health care process. It is not meant to be a comprehensive treatise on managed care, nor is it just another text about short-term group psychotherapy. The content is based on an assumption of mine that group psychotherapy will become an ever-increasing form of mental health care under any system of managed care, public or private.

I am of the opinion that there will be a "marriage," albeit in some cases an arranged marriage, between the requirements, regulations, and restrictions imposed by managed care and the technical flexibility, facility with time adjustments, and ability to reach almost any patient population that group therapy provides. Although this "match" seems apparent to me, there is virtually nothing in the scientific, self-help, managed care, or popular literature that actually explicates issues at the interface between managed mental health care and contemporary group psychotherapy.

The book is divided into four major parts. The first deals with a general overview of both managed care principles and the tenets of brief group psychotherapy. The chapters in Part II, on clinical issues, form the bulk of the text and are geared toward the provider. This segment of the book explicates the process of creating a managed care group. It is deliberately clinical in its orientation and is designed to describe the "nuts and bolts" of how to compose and conduct a therapeutic group in the context of managed mental health care.

Part III concerns itself with special issues: loose ends, people, and places that do not fit easily into the managed care group model. A sampling of topics in this part of the book includes the issues raised for the chronically mentally ill patient, factors associated with hospitalization, and patients diagnosed as having specific problems that require innovative thinking in order that appropriate models of group treatment may be designed.

The concluding group of chapters, in Part IV, Documenting the Group Experience and Evaluating Outcomes, focuses on managed care reporting methods, assessment of outcome in time-effective group psychotherapy, ethical issues, and future trends in both managed mental health care and group treatment.

Clinical guides, evaluation instruments, and suggested forms to be used in conjunction with managed care group work are sprinkled throughout the text in the hope of simplifying and clarifying for the clinician/provider the task of leading a managed care group. Appendix A presents Ethical Guidelines from the American Group Psychotherapy Association. Appendix B includes instruction guidelines for completing the Eligibility Form provided by the National Registry of Certified Group Psychotherapists.

Since time is of the essence in the managed care philosophy, I have made an effort to keep the book pragmatically oriented with enough theoretical and scientific background as needed to explain the rationale for the various suggestions given throughout the text. My hope is that this book will serve as a clinical guide for those interested in expanding their skills into the managed care arena.

Part I

Introduction to Managed Care and the Brief Group Therapies

1

General Principles of Managed Mental Health Care in the Clinical Setting

"It was the best of times, it was the worst of times." Is this a quotation from Charles Dickens in 1859 or is it the sentiment expressed by those in the field of mental health care in the mid 1990s?

There is a revolution in contemporary health care. This has contributed to a great sense of hope and optimism on the part of some while simultaneously engendering a state of fear and despair in others involved in various parts of the health care delivery system. Health care reform is in a state of such dramatic flux that it has virtually polarized, if not paralyzed, clinicians, administrators, insurers, politicians, and the American public.

What seems certain is that dramatic changes in both the forms and mechanisms through which health care services are transmitted are already in place in many circles and will continue to evolve as greater experience with new formats is accumulated. The implications for mental health care in particular are profound.

Essential issues of cost containment, time restrictions, evaluation of the efficacy and outcome of different therapeutic interventions, consumer satisfaction, and appropriate financing of these changes are on the minds of virtually all those involved on any significant level in the field of mental health.

Ideally, the obvious goal is to meet the challenge of providing excellent clinical care to large groups of people in a reasonable time frame at a price affordable to all. In recent years, innovative and creative models of mental health care delivery have emerged and have been

3

broadly subsumed under the rubric of "managed mental health care." The concept of managed care has been interpreted and implemented in so many different forms that it has yet to take unified shape and has left a considerable gap in both the understanding of and degree of comfort with what exactly the term "managed care" means.

Although some of the language of managed care has found its way into common clinical parlance, it does not necessarily reflect a corresponding degree of sophistication, comfort, or true appreciation on the part of the majority of practitioners regarding what this will actually mean in terms of treating people with emotional disorders. To overstate the case, perhaps the dilemma for the practitioner is whether mental health care reform in general, and the various formats of managed care in particular, will be the best or worst of modern times.

Those on the positive side of the issue welcome change, which they regard as long overdue in the streamlining of an outmoded, costly, inefficient, and discriminatory mental health care system. In addition, many advocates of managed care cite not only the fiscal benefits of a new system but the simultaneous challenges and opportunities it opens up for creative solutions to many long-standing frustrations for both the clinician and patient in this milieu.

Others are not so optimistic about the emerging trends in managed care. Practitioners with a traditional point of view are worried that, from an altruistic standpoint, patient care will be inferior and the client-therapist relationship irreparably damaged by managed care. On the personal side, there is almost a sense of "environmental paranoia" in the hearts and minds of clinicians who envision diminished income; greater intrusion into their work by employers, administrators, and insurers; and strong reservations about participation in a plan about which they will have little say in the conduct of their professional work.

The current trend is reminiscent of the prevailing clinical climate that followed the movement towards deinstitutionalization of chronically mentally ill patients in the late 1960s and early 1970s. Mental health care providers found themselves charged with the task of serving the psychological needs of enormous numbers of patients without a coexisting feeling of being experienced enough in techniques designed to meet the unique needs of this patient population. This, in tandem with concerns about inadequate funding, training, understaffing and lack of sound research data on the subject, created a clinical climate of demoralization, despair, and disappointment.

It was at this period in the modern history of the mental health movement that group psychotherapy emerged as a promising element in the service of resolving many of these pressing treatment problems. The appeal of therapeutic groups was threefold: More people could be accommodated in the group setting than in the dyadic or individual therapy model, less expenditure of staff time was required because of the high patient-to-clinician ratio in groups, and the cost of group therapy was about one-third to one-half that of individual long-term psychotherapy.

We are at a similar crossroads now. The current crisis in the American health care system demands a search for treatment efforts that are relatively brief; more specifically symptom-focused (rather than vague and globally focused); and clearly defined and documentable, lending themselves to scientific study of treatment outcome and efficacy (Feldman & Fitzpatrick, 1992; Goodman, Brown, & Deitz, 1992).

The central focus of the text will be to address issues at the interface between managed mental health care and group psychotherapy. After a general orientation and discussion of managed care principles, the thrust of the volume will be pragmatic and clinically oriented, with the goal of providing the reader with an increased understanding of the rationale for the selection, organization, and actual conduct of group psychotherapy in the context of the managed care setting.

SCOPE OF THE PROBLEM: "FACTS AND FIGURES"

Clearly, one, if not the central, motive for overhauling and revamping the health care system in the United States has an economic basis. Costs of providing mental health and substance abuse services have escalated yearly and the prospect of continuation of the same system shows no signs of changing these trends.

Current estimates state that approximately 37 million Americans are without health insurance and a substantial additional number are underinsured. As a corollary to this, the term "access to care" includes still more people who, for a variety of reasons, are not able to take advantage of the full range of benefits available to them under the present system. Cost shifting becomes another concern in instances where those citizens who are uninsured must enter the health care system through the expensive doors of emergency rooms all over the country.

Cost containment is of paramount importance to all. In 1993, the cost of providing health care under the current system was estimated at more than $800 billion, or 14.9% of the nation's Gross National Product (*Psychiatric News*, April, 1993). Reliable reports (Report of the Advisory Council to the National Institute of Mental Health, 1993) suggest that about 10%, or $80 billion, is spent annually for the direct treatment of all mental disorders. In 1990, the cost of direct treatment and long-term nursing home care of people defined as having "severe" mental disorders was $27 billion out of a total health care budget of $670 billion for that fiscal year.

Further evidence for the skyrocketing costs of health care comes from the business sector. In the 1960s, employers spent about 4 to 8 cents of each dollar of profit on health care whereas the figures for 1990 estimate the cost as 50 cents per dollar and future projections indicate that by the year 2000 this cost will approach 60 cents (Goodman et al., 1992).

The figures are staggering and have caused many people to take steps towards improving the situation with respect to the care of the mentally ill. In devising an improved and effective plan for treating psychiatrically impaired Americans, one must be aware of some of the following salient observations gleaned from an analysis of current data regarding mental health statistics. The "full spectrum of mental disorders" (using DSM-III-R criteria) affects 22% of the adult population in a given year, according to the American Psychiatric Association. Furthermore, "severe" mental disorders–defined as schizophrenia, manic depressive illness and serious forms of depression, panic disorder, and obsessive compulsive states–affect 2.8% of the adult population, numbering about five million people. This group accounts for 25% of all federal disability payments (SSI and SSDI).

Other relevant factors that have a bearing on mental health care reform include the realization that 10.9% of the population currently seek some form of mental health treatment in a given year. Of this group, only 50% meet the criteria for having a mental disorder. In addition, less than 7% of the population have symptoms that last for one year or longer and only 9% report some disability associated with a primary mental disorder. In terms of utilization of available mental health care services, some interesting findings emerge in reference to the setting in which people seek and actually obtain treatment for mental disorders. The general health care segment accounts for 43% of visits, while the mental health specialty sector sees 40%. Some 28% of those looking for mental health care or intervention do so in the voluntary health sector (American Psychiatric Association, 1993).

One obvious conclusion to be drawn from this data is that the mentally ill in our society comprise a significant percentage of the health care consumers of services. Any reform plan that makes economic sense must address the pressing needs of this segment of our national populace. Despite these facts, many of the proposed new formats for implementing health care reform reflect, at best, a disproportionate, and, at worst, a discriminatory use of the health care dollars spent for mental health and substance abuse services. Those who advocate such legislation are, in effect, creating a prejudicial situation favoring the medically ill over the mentally ill.

OVERVIEW OF PROPOSED MENTAL HEALTH REFORM PLANS

An ideal mental health care reform plan would contain elements that take into account economic, social, moral, and ethical factors. Even at this early stage of health care reform, it is easy to see that this seemingly desirable model appears naive when one actually examines the contents of prospective changes in mental health care benefits currently being entertained.

Since the field of health care reform is rapidly becoming densely populated by a host of new proposals, it is beyond the scope of this chapter to review each prospective plan in detail. Instead, we will review the major issues affecting patterns of mental health care, coverage, and treatment. The primary focus will be on elements of various reform plans that are controversial and what the implications of each is likely to be for the actual practice of mental health care in the future. In the broadest sense, managed mental health care or managed competition can be defined as "a variety of systems and strategies aimed at marshalling appropriate clinical and financial resources to ensure needed care for consumers. Its central feature is the heightened activity of employers and insurers in defining what kind and how much care is needed and, therefore, is reimbursable" (Winegar, 1992).

"Managed competition," a term used most frequently to describe the type of plan favored by the federal administration, "aims at blending the competitive forces of a free market with some degree of government regulation. Advocates believe this approach will control spiraling health care costs while fostering quality care. Health planners appear to agree that, among other features, such a plan is likely to include: organized systems of care, health insurance purchasing cooperatives and a National Health Board" (*Psychiatric News*, April, 1993).

For purposes of simplicity, the array of health care reform proposals will be discussed from the point of view of the impact of core elements of these plans upon patients and clinicians. One way of conceptualizing the key issues involved in both comprehensive medical reform proposals and those portions that have greatest import for the field of mental health is to identify central characteristics of each and to arbitrarily group them into six broad categories: plan structure, access to coverage, benefit packages, financing of the plan, the implications for practitioners, and how different proposals deal with the issue of malpractice.

It is easiest to take a look at established models or proposals and compare and contrast how a typical reform plan deals with each of the six different categories and the salient features involved in restructuring or reorganizing mental health care benefits. The range of proposals suggested by officials holding public office has been so numerous that they can serve as a "laboratory" for studying key elements in different plans. For purposes of this text, it does not matter which specific plan may be eventually adopted. Instead, these plans are to be viewed as prototypes of managed mental health care reform and as such serve as excellent examples of what goes into the thinking process in composing such plans. There are many state and private plans that currently exist and still more under development, so it would be impossible to cover the full range of options potentially available to the consumer in this brief survey format.

The range of options with regard to how a reform plan is structured refers to what form of managed competition they do or do not advocate and how the managed care plan will be implemented. The original Health Security Act, also known as "the Clinton plan," espoused a system of managed competition in which employers and/or consumers purchase coverage through state or corporate health alliances that negotiate with a variety of health plans or providers of services. This plan would be overseen by a National Health Board and allows individual states to elect to choose alternative systems.

Other proposals may be viewed as variations on this basic theme. Some plans, like the American Health Security Act (McDermott HR 1200), use a model more akin to the Canadian health care system, involving single-payer, government run national health insurance, with the states bearing the administrative responsibilities. There is disagreement over whether or not individuals should be mandated to purchase health insurance among the different plans under consideration (Cooper, HR3222; Chafee, S1770). A number of these plans accent the role played by large business, with some encouraging employers to set up their own health plans or health care cooperatives.

The use of medical savings accounts and/or tax credits to help individuals and families to purchase health insurance is another aspect of structure in some new health care models. (Affordable Health Care Now Act, Michel HR3080; Consumer Choice Health Security Act, Nickles, S1743). Lastly, the issue of creating a mechanism by which financial contribution between employer and employee can be effectuated has been addressed in several ways. Proposed mechanisms vary from a form that would set requirements for individuals to buy basic health coverage and have the employer withhold payments for the premiums from the employee's paycheck, to the encouragement of independent insurance purchasing groups. Risk pools to lessen insurer risk and subsidization plans for the poor to be better able to afford adequate health care coverage are also common structural themes currently under debate under a system of universal coverage.

Access to health care is the second area of study. Most plans are in agreement about providing expanded health care coverage in some form for all citizens while excluding illegal aliens from the program. The range of options runs the gamut from mandatory universal coverage to no universal coverage with alternative choices, such as the requirement for employers to offer insurance without a corresponding obligation to pay for it. The vehicles of some form of vouchers and/or tax credits to help implement affordability of the various plans are currently under consideration in many sectors. The differences among prospective plans become even more apparent in the inclusion, exclusion, or reduction of benefits from Medicare, Medicaid, CHAMPUS, Veterans Administration, Indian Health Service, and other federally funded programs.

A closely related third general theme is found in the combination of benefits contained in each plan or "package." The most generous plans guarantee comprehensive medical coverage but are less forthcoming about where mental health and substance abuse services are concerned. The Clinton plan is a prototype of this model, offering comprehensive coverage of hospitals, doctors, and prescription drugs, with only limited mental health and substance abuse benefits. Specific restrictions regarding the number of inpatient days, how much intensive residential treatment and community services, and whether or not a plan permits the right to "trade off" benefits such as inpatient days in exchange for greater outpatient coverage are contained in virtually all plans under study. Similarly, most proponents of these plans suggest that the benefit policies cannot be canceled or denied and also propose some form of cost-sharing plan for payment of psychotherapeutic services.

The fourth factor, the financing of health care, is perhaps the most complex and most emotionally charged subject in the field of health care reform. For the purposes of this text, a limited overview will outline some examples of how the various plans will be paid for and who will do the paying in each instance. The Clinton model is one in which the employer is mandated to cover the employee and to provide some hardship subsidies. Payment will come from several sources. One vehicle is via selected tax increases such as a higher tobacco tax or so-called "sin taxes." There would be limitations on the extent to which monies paid towards health care policy premiums would be tax deductible. Curtailing some Medicare and Medicaid benefits would help defer the cost of the new plan.

In this format, the financing would be overseen by a National Health Board, which would also have the power to set budgets, regulate premium amounts, and establish caps on spending under the plan.

Alternative thinkers propose other ways of financing the health care budget by changing the ways in which state tax dollars are allocated from federal funds. They suggest use of a matching fund arrangement where states will contribute 15–20% of the cost. Some propose that states be given the ability to negotiate with private health care providers to establish a fee structure that will depend upon which health care plan is ultimately adopted as a means of reducing the economic burden attendant to new health care legislation.

Regardless of the eventual form health care provision takes, it is certain that some form of innovative or creative financing plan must accompany it.

The fifth area, and the one which most directly affects mental health professionals who actually treat psychologically impaired patients, is the potential practice implications that result as an inevitable by-product of any new system of managed mental health care service delivery and financing.

It appears that there will be a shift in health care towards an ever increasing role for the primary physician. A patient's first contact with any new system is likely to be with a nonpsychiatric physician who will be in a position to evaluate whether or not mental health services are indicated and who shall provide them. This phenomenon, often referred to as the "gatekeeper" function, aims at reducing unnecessary referrals for psychological treatment and will undoubtedly result in the use of brief interventions and increased use of psychotropic medications as central features of treatment plans of the future.

Along with this emphasis on primary care, there is also a strong sentiment among proponents of new health care plans that the best way to reach these goals is through the expanded role of the Health Maintenance Organization, Preferred Provider Organization, or other organized, accredited provider network administered by a Managed Mental Health Care firm (MMHC). An MMHC firm is an entity best conceptualized as an organization that monitors and oversees the workings of the provider network.

The interplay between the MMHC and the network is as follows: Clinicians who are members of the network agree to the MMHC firm's clinical guidelines or standards. Members also agree to discounted fee arrangements. In addition, providers agree to accept pre-set fees for services rendered, to comply with the quality control systems used by the MMHC, and to utilize the MMHC as a source for prospective patients.

From a practical point of view, it is important for clinicians to consider whether or not to join such networks in order to maintain a steady influx of prospective patients since the MMHC will play an ever increasing role as the conduit through which referrals are made to mental health specialists. As Winegar (1992) aptly predicts, "Clinicians will need increased familiarity with short-term, brief therapy techniques and interventions, which are philosophically compatible with managed care values and benefit constraints" (p. 123).

In almost all plans, patients have a choice of their physician as long as he or she is a member of the network. When the issue of mental health referral arises, the choice process for the patient is generally restricted to those mental health specialists within the network who are referred by the primary care physician.

The monitoring of treatment and outcome is central to virtually all programs seriously under consideration. There is an enormous desire on the part of government, insurers, MMHC firms, and businesses to ensure that the process of mental health treatment is efficient and documentable. Time and expense are the two most obvious causes for concern among these groups.

Before leaving the subject of practice implications, it should be mentioned that most plans advocate an increase in the training of future primary care practitioners and include a significantly smaller budget for the training and education of future mental health specialists.

Factor number six in this brief review of proposed health care plans as they relate to the clinician is the important issue of how possible malpractice issues will be handled. The provisions of a model like the Clinton plan advocate mandatory alternative dispute resolution and a cap on both attorney fees and awards in suits. There would also be public access to a National Data Bank and research on protection for physicians, in part by exploring legal issues involved in enterprise liability. Some plans simply do not include or address the malpractice question, but most of them make an effort to identify and weed out substandard practitioners through the use of some form of utilization review process.

It is axiomatic that the proponents of the new health care plans view them in a favorable and constructive light and feel that they have much to offer in improving the problems in the health care system. There are, however, a substantial number of voices emerging from both inside and outside the MMMC community who raise questions with critical consequences for the future of both mental health care and substance abuse treatment. In order to present a fair and balanced review of both sides of the mental health care reform issue, some of the points raised by critics of the new system will be highlighted briefly.

The most vociferous challenges come from practitioners who have grave concerns about the future of mental health care in this country on several fronts . McCaughey (1993) has summarized many of these potentially troublesome issues, using the Clinton plan model as the foundation for her assertions. She identifies seven issues that could clearly make health care reform backfire in its mission to improve conditions and, indeed, may be considered anywhere from shortsighted to dangerous.

(1) Most Americans will not be able to keep their current physicians or buy the kind of insurance that 77% of Americans now choose. (2) It will be hard to buy additional insurance. (3) Seeing a specialist and paying for it out-of-pocket will be almost impossible. (4) Price controls will make private practice unfeasible. (5) Americans have been told that the quality of health care will not decline. Many experts believe it will. (6) The plan also takes away from HMO users the legal protection that many state lawmakers believe they should have. (7) The plan's biggest surprise is who bears the cost of universal health coverage. (pp. 12–13)

A most dramatic summation of the position of those who oppose proposed health care reform is contained in McCaughey's opinion that "The Clinton plan is coercive. It takes personal choices away from patients and families, and imposes a system of financing health care based on regional alliances that will make racial tensions fester and produce political struggles and lawsuits to shirk the cost of medical care for the urban poor" (p. 13).

The battle lines have been drawn and supporters on both sides have expressed their views clearly and emphatically. While it is not currently known what form health care will ultimately take, what does seem self-evident is that, as Dorwart (1994, p. 43) puts it, "For better or worse, the reliance on organized systems of care, on a variety of network-model practices and on services provided in health plans that include hospitals, community clinics and physician group practices will increase dramatically." Furthermore, "Under health care reform, there will be economic incentives to reduce duplication of services, coordinate service systems for individuals with severe illnesses and to consolidate public and private funds including Medicaid programs."

The essential features of any new health care system are well categorized in the American Medical Association's Health System Reform Proposal For Action (1994). The key elements are: degree of coverage, health care professional's role or involvement, personal liability reform, quality of care, freedom of choice, cost containment, simplifying the system, collaboration among various members of the treatment team, and financing health care reform. The above noted factors form a useful framework for understanding the practical impact of any newly created system of health care reform. A fuller discussion of the ramifications of these plans as they relate to actual practice will be incorporated into the body of this text and will be explored further in Chapter 14.

MANAGED MENTAL HEALTH CARE: A NEW VOCABULARY

Along with the rapid influx of proposals for renovation of the health care system has come a new lexicon of terms and a "language of managed care." Many of these terms have already been interwoven into this chapter but no initial overview of managed care would be complete without defining a few terms commonly used (and misused). Even more important, this will help facilitate effective communication among all those in the system by making them "fluent" in a common health care language.

Some terms are new and others merely provide labels for "old wine in new bottles." Examples of the latter are to be found in the substitution of provider for clinician/therapist, consumer for patient/client, and payor for insurer/employer.

Since health care reform has much to do with business and money, many commonly used terms originate in the world of business and/or economics. "Capitation" is a way of controlling costs of mental health care. In a capitated system, for example, a consumer is assigned to a provider who receives a flat payment for each member of the population seen each month. In return for this per capita payment, the provider assumes the obligation to provide all services required by plan members as defined by their benefit plan. There are also capitated plans in which an organized provider group such as an HMO or independent practitioner group contracts under an arrangement whereby the providers decide on the distribution of mental health services within the confines of the capitated budget.

Monitoring of treatment is done through a process called "case management." Although this will be discussed at length in Chapter 13, a simple definition of case management is one in which clinical information is evaluated to first determine (precertification review) and then to ensure the medical necessity of treatment and the provision of effective, quality care (concurrent review) through the most cost-effective means. Often a review of records or treatment plans of discharged patients is conducted and is called a retrospective review.

One final term that serves to illustrate a new concept emanating from managed care is the notion of "point of service" (POS). A point-of-service plan provides financial incentives to members who elect to have their treatment services performed by "preferred providers." These are in-network providers whose services carry higher rates of reimbursement than if the consumer chose to see someone out-of-network.

Throughout the text, managed care "jargon" will be explained as needed in order to help demystify the terminology of this complex and often confusing field. For the sake of clarity, the chapters to follow will deliberately take the liberty of deciding when to use of traditional terminology and when managed care terminology would be preferable in whichever way best serves to illustrate or illuminate the clinical points to be made.

This short review of managed care principles sets the stage to proceed to a discussion of time-limited or brief group psychotherapy. Brief group therapy is a treatment modality that will form the crux of this text because of its superb ability to operationalize many of the basic theoretical tenets of managed mental health care and transpose them into the actual clinical setting, thereby helping immeasurably in attaining the positive goals of mental health care reform.

2

Brief Group Psychotherapy: Historical Perspectives and Contemporary Trends

In order to fully appreciate the applications of the brief group therapy model to managed mental health care treatment, it is helpful to have an understanding of the evolution and the typology of present day group practices. See Table 1.

Contemporary group psychotherapeutic methods are derived from two primary influences: short-term individual psychotherapy and brief group psychotherapy. Although these therapies are discussed separately, their historical development overlapped and one can be viewed as enhancing the progress of the other.

In a strict chronological sense, individual psychotherapy predates group therapy, starting with the birth of psychoanalysis before 1900. Despite the fact that even Freud, in his *Studies on Hysteria*, and later, in the mid-1920s, Rank and Ferenczi demonstrated a willingness to try to tailor the length of the treatment to needs of the given patient, it is really not until the end of World War II that psychoanalytically or psychodynamically oriented psychotherapists and theorists began to employ time adjustments as an integral aspect of their work.

In 1944, Grinker and Spiegel wrote about their method of "brief psychotherapy" in the treatment of psychiatric casualties from World War II. Lindemann also described brief individual work around issues of grief in the same year. Alexander and French are generally credited as key figures in modern psychoanalytic circles as practitioners who valued "flexibility" in their psychotherapeutic work with patients. This orientation opened the door for further experimentation with the use of variable time frames in psychodynamically oriented individual psychotherapy.

In the early 1960s, one really sees the explosion in the theory and practice of short-term individual psychotherapies. As Bloom (1992) notes, "Starting in 1963, coincident with the formal beginning of the community mental health movement, a series of major volumes began appearing that described and evaluated what has since come to be called planned short-term psychotherapy" (p. 3). Authors whose names have now become familiar in the mental health field were beginning their pioneering efforts to establish a greater understanding of what they had noticed empirically in their clinical work. Bellak, Wolberg, and Malan are examples of three representative figures who attempted to move away from a literature that was primarily anecdotal and descriptive to one that delineated a clear rationale for the use of these brief techniques.

The 1970s saw further advances in brief individual work as reflected in the writings of Sifneos (1992), Davanloo (1980), Budman and Gurman 1988), Klerman et al. (1984), Beck (1979), and others. The net effect of this body of work was to lend credence to the use of brief psychotherapeutic interventions by explicating the actual process of what transpires in sessions, by showing how to arrive at attainable goals, and, perhaps most important to those skeptical of brief therapy, by establishing methods for evaluating outcome and efficacy of time-limited approaches. Specific similarities and differences among these different "schools" of brief therapy will be discussed later in this chapter.

To return to the parallel developments in the field of brief group psychotherapy, one must revisit New England at the turn of the century. The modern historical origins of group psychotherapy are generally credited to Joseph Pratt (1922), an internist who worked with tuberculosis patients during their notoriously long convalesencent periods. Pratt held "classes" for patients in which lectures and information about their illness would be disseminated. Although this activity began as a way of filling time for patients, it resulted in several significant serendipitous findings. Pratt and his staff noticed that the patients who attended the classes seemed to be less demoralized and/or depressed and clearly were more cooperative in participating in their individual medical treatment plans.

TABLE 1*
Typology of Groups

	Self-Help Group
Size	Large (size often unlimited)
Leadership	1. Peer leader or recovered substance abuser 2. Leadership is earned status over time 3. Implicit hierarchical leadership structure
Membership Participation	Voluntary
Group Governed	Self-governing
Content	1. Environmental factors, no examination of group interaction 2. Emphasis on similarities among members 3. "Here and now" focus
Screening Interview	None
Group Processes	Universalization, empathy, affective sharing, education, public statement of problem (self-disclosure), mutual affirmation, morale building, catharsis, immediate positive feedback, high degrees of persuasiveness
Outside Socialization	1. Encouraged strongly 2. Construction of social network is actively sought
Goals	1. Positive goal setting, behaviorally oriented 2. Focus on the "group as a whole" and the similarities among members
Leader Activity	1. Educator/role model catalyst for learning 2. Less member-to-leader distance
Use of Interpretation or Psychodynamic Techniques	No
Confidentiality	Anonymity preserved
Sponsorship Program	Yes (usually same sex)
Deselection	1. Members may leave group at their own choosing 2. Members may avoid self-disclosure or discussion of any subject
Involvement in Other Groups/Programs	Yes
Time Factors	Unlimited group participation possible over years
Frequency of Meetings	Active encouragement of daily participation

*Adapted from Spitz & Rosecan (1987). *Cocaine abuse: New directions in treatment and research.* (pp. 162–163). New York: Brunner/Mazel.

Psychotherapy Group	Managed Care Group
Small (8–15 members)	Small (8–10 members)
1. Mental health professional 2. Self-appointed leadership 3. Formal hierarchical leadership structure	Professional mental health leadership
Voluntary and involuntary	Voluntary
Leader governed	Leader governed
1. Examination of intragroup behavior and extragroup factors 2. Emphasis on differentiation among members over time 3. "Here and now" plus historical focus	1. Examination of intragroup issues and transfer of learning to life outside group 2. "Here and now" focus
Always	Always and strong pre-group orientation
Cohesion, mutual identification confrontation, education, catharsis, use of group pressure re: abstinence and retention of group membership	Cohesion, peer support, homogeneous group factors
1. Cautious re: extragroup contact 2. Intermember networking is optional	1. Depending on nature of group 2. Usually is optional
1. Ambitious goals: immediate problems plus individual personality issues 2. Individual as well as group focus	1. Crisis resolution 2. Specific target symptoms or behavior 3. Life-cycle issues
1. Responsible for therapeutic group experience 2. More member-to-leader distance	Leader very active in structuring group experience
Yes	Usually not (exception-high functioning groups)
Strongly emphasized	Strongly emphasized
No	No
1. Predetermined minimal term of commitment to group membership 2. Avoidance of discussion seen as "resistance"	1. Members may be screened out during orientation phase or in first 1–2 sessions
Yes–eclectic models No–psychodynamic models	Yes
Often time-limited experiences	Strict time limitations
Meets less frequently (often once or twice weekly)	Usually once per week; cognitive/behavioral and in-patient groups meet more frequently

Others, including Lazell (1921) and Marsh (1931), learned of Pratt's work, applied the method specifically to inpatients suffering from psychiatric illness, and observed similar results. An awareness of the power and dynamics of groups was evident in Freud's (1921) *Group Psychology and the Analysis of the Ego.* However, like individual therapy, groups did not begin their exponential growth until the mid-1940s.

With the psychological carnage wreaked by the war, a situation arose in which the number of people requiring psychological attention far outnumbered the professionals available to care for them. As a consequence, it seemed evident that greater numbers of people in need of help could be seen in groups; this approach would thereby help solve the problem of the relative shortage of psychological caregivers. This led to a rash of experimentation with the group model, with therapists basically trying to adapt psychoanalytic or psychodynamic principles to the small group setting.

Alexander Wolf, whose name is virtually synonymous with psychoanalysis in groups, J.L. Moreno, credited as the creator of the psychodrama technique, and Nathan Ackerman, the founder of modern family therapy, were all working simultaneously to discover the therapeutic potential and diverse applicability of working in small groups.

Kurt Lewin (1951), a social psychologist, developed his "field theory," an idea that suggests that, "The group to which an individual belongs is the ground for his perceptions, his feelings and his actions...it is the ground of the social group that gives to the individual his figured character" (Allport, 1948). While Lewin was not a clinician but more a theoretician interested in group dynamics, he believed that "people could change themselves and adapt to external demands if they faced the change as part of a group that was actively guiding the change process. The best technique for achieving successful change was to engage a small group in studying how to bring about the changes to which each individual was committed" (Sabin, 1981).

From this point in Lewin's theory, it is a short step towards the foundation for the sensitivity, "T"-groups, and encounter experiences that were emblematic of group work in the 1960s. Experimentation with modification of different variables in group, including group leadership, membership, size, focus, and *time* (both time-limited and time-extended group formats), led to a deeper understanding of the limits of group experiences and to an appreciation of the deleterious as well as beneficial aspects of group experiences.

Lieberman, Yalom, and Miles's (1973) landmark study of encounter groups shed light on critical issues of leadership style, participant selection, and psychiatric casualties that emerged from a range of sensitivity and encounter group formats. Yalom's (1975) publication of one of the first single authored texts with an interpersonal, existential, and "here-and-now" orientation paved the way for proponents of brief group experiences to have a firm footing in scientific, clinical group research as a basis for their innovations with time factors in therapeutic groups.

Budman (1981) was one of the first practitioners of brief individual psychotherapy to try the application of the short-term techniques in the milieu of the psychotherapy group. More recently, MacKenzie (1990) has published extensively on the topic of "time-limited" group psychotherapy and has outlined a method deemed appropriate for treating a broad range of emotional problems in an expeditious and efficient fashion.

The confluence of forces in the fields of individual, group, family, and marital therapy over the years has resulted in a greater degree of choice for both patient and therapist. This becomes critical when the therapeutic task is conducted in the managed care arena. Instead of feeling handcuffed, therapists now have available to them a broad array of therapeutic interventions that increase rather than restrict options in planning comprehensive psychiatric treatment for the managed care patient/consumer.

The aforementioned historical efforts are far from irrelevant or of passing academic interest. They delineate the genesis of significant theories and techniques that have been updated, refined, and incorporated into a creative and pragmatic psychological armamentarium that is broadly subsumed under the label of the brief group therapies.

BRIEF THERAPIES: RATIONALE AND GOALS

This section will center on themes related to the theoretical underpinnings for the expressed advantages of short-term psychotherapies and on a discussion of their commonalities of purpose. Later in this chapter, some of the differences among the prevailing forms of brief psychotherapy will form the basis for subsequent discussion.

Several social, economic, and psychotherapeutic elements have created a climate over time that has moved in the direction of briefer, more focused, and goal-directed treatment. An analysis of some of these seemingly diverse factors reveals that some distinct trends were, and currently are, developing that call for psychotherapy with a clearly defined and planned time limit in the future.

The economic incentive to contain the escalating costs of mental health services is a pressing social and monetary issue. This has increased the already existing sense of urgency to find newer and shorter ways of working with the mentally ill. While the financial motives are self-evident, what may be more subtle but equally important are the shifting views concerning the conduct of psychotherapy in general and of brief psychotherapy in particular.

Research data on outcome in psychotherapy and increased experience with time-limited therapies have caused a shift away from traditional ways of thinking about psychological treatment in the minds of many in the mental health field. Bloom (1992) attributes the growing interest in planned short-term therapy to five factors: "(1) acceptance of limited therapeutic goals, (2) emphasis in ego psychology on strengths as well as weakness of the client, (3) impact of behavior modification techniques, (4) increased centrality of crisis theory and crisis intervention in service delivery system planning, and (5) greater attention being paid to current precipitating circumstances in contrast to past predisposing circumstances" (p. 8).

Much of this sentiment is echoed and expanded upon in Pardes and Pincus's (1981) list of factors that they feel have focused the attention of mental health care providers on short-term psychotherapies. In addition to underscoring the acceptance of circumscribed goals in treatment planning, they go on to cite the following as other influential forces in creating the trend toward brief psychotherapy: "the increasing development of an array of varied treatments along with a rapprochement of different therapeutic approaches; advances in classification of emotional disorders; the growing realization that lengthy treatments often do not meet the needs of particular populations; an increasing concern with the costs of treatment combined with increasing access to treatment; and the growth of pre-paid health plans with limited psychiatric benefits" (p. 12).

Although these lists are far from comprehensive, they do capture the essence of the rationale for the use of short-term methods in the dyadic and group settings. The starting point for the implementation of many of these principles into a form that is clinically viable begins with the orientation of the clinician and how his or her point of view influences the type of therapy chosen in any given case. With this idea in mind, it would be helpful for us to clarify some of the key points of difference between therapists with a long-term orientation and those with a more time-limited focus.

Budman and Gurman (1988) helped shed light on the question of differences between therapists with a long-term orientation and those with a penchant for short-term work. They described some essential differences in orientation, point of view, and actual clinical practice along a number of parameters. The short-term therapist prefers "pragmatism and parsimony" and does not seek change in basic character structure as a goal of treatment. Moreover, exponents of the brief therapies see the possibilities for change as being less confined to early childhood experiences, but instead prefer a view that assumes that significant events, experiences, traumas, and learning can occur at any point in the life cycle, from infancy to old age. This adult developmental model is characteristic of Budman's approach.

From a clinical focus standpoint, both the long-term and the brief therapy practitioner pay careful attention to the patient's current complaints, with the former more likely to view "symptoms" as evidence of more serious psychopathology and the latter more likely to include an assessment of and emphasis on patient strengths and resources. The brief therapist makes the assumption that the shortest and least radical interventions are the most useful and that they will result in benefits continuing outside of and after the formal therapeutic experience is over. This concept closely parallels Yalom's emphasis on the "transfer of learning" factor in therapeutic groups wherein the group member is encouraged to apply in-group insights into his/her life outside the group.

This maxim helps to further distinguish between the orientation of the long term therapist, who also hopes for changes to take place outside of regular sessions, but is usually more wedded to the idea that more sessions and longer time spent in therapy will enhance this process, and the brief therapist who puts more stock in using therapy as a "staging area" for change rather than the "mission control" model preferred by long-term therapists. The latter view the therapist's strengths as paramount and thus encourage the patient to rely on the process of therapy as a guide for negotiating their "flight paths" through life.

The brief therapist never talks in the language of "cure," but rather in the language of "change." In this respect, exponents of the brief therapies see people as in a constant state of change over time and work with the presenting problem or expressed area of emotional urgency in the patient's life at the present time. They are less likely to focus on past history unless there is a repetitive pattern of behavior that has been present for many years and requires attention. Still, the orientation of the brief therapist is to "treat" the current manifestations of the patient's problem as they manifest themselves in a "here and now" context.

The role of formal diagnosis is noteworthy in the difference in weight given to it by both traditional and contemporary methods. With the recent publication (1994) of the *Diagnostic and Statistical Manual of Mental Disorders, Fourth Edition*, by the American Psychiatric Association, renewed interest in clarification and precision in making psychiatric diagnoses has accentuated this issue even more. Both short-term and long-term therapies value any information of a diagnostic nature that will eventually have great bearing on treatment planning. As such, long-term and short-term therapists are similar in the sense that both pay careful attention to data relevant to psychopathology and DSM-IV classification. The primary point of departure between the two is the strong belief by practitioners of brief psychotherapy that an assessment of the patient's strengths and resources is as relevant as the deficit/illness model of evaluation and diagnosis, if not more so.

Brief therapists view time factors as limited, not limitless or open-ended. They attempt to communicate to the patient a sense of commonly agreed upon, realistic goals for solutions to troublesome issues in the patient's current life circumstances. By structuring the therapeutic experience as finite, the brief therapist conveys an implicit and explicit set of expectations on the part of clinician and patient that change is possible within a fixed time span. The clinical manifestations of this stance will be evident in later chapters which address the actual conduct of brief group psychotherapy with respect to how time factors can be employed constructively.

Lastly, one of the central differences between the long-term and short-term therapist revolves around how each sees the relative value of being in therapy versus being on one's own. Traditional therapies of longer duration have expressed the position that the ongoing therapeutic relationship between patient and therapist is critical to therapeutic success. Brief therapists understand the value of a good therapeutic alliance, but tend to encourage less dependency on the therapist or on the process of psychotherapy and more emphasis on life outside of therapy.

As Budman and Gurman (1988) have put it, "being in the world is seen as more important than being in therapy. Most brief therapists are present-oriented. They are interested in emphasizing current relationships, present-centered problems, and ongoing life situations. This type of orientation has major implications for determining the style of therapist intervention and the use of significant others in the treatment process" (p. 15). While the authors were addressing the individual therapy model, the same orientation has far-reaching implications for brief group psychotherapy as well.

For an excellent review of the similarities and differences among the various "schools" of brief individual psychotherapy and a thoughtful analysis of the techniques employed by each, the reader is referred to Bloom's (1992) superb text on planned short-term psychotherapies.

Since the main thrust of this book concerns itself with the application of short-term group methods in the managed care setting, the latter part of this chapter will focus on two critical issues: the interface between brief individual psychotherapy and brief group therapy, and some general principles common to most brief group therapies.

Roy MacKenzie, a pioneer in the field of time-limited group psychotherapy, has suggested that in order to best understand the overlapping areas of agreement among practitioners of brief individual psychotherapy and those who employ brief techniques in the group milieu, some of the language and terminology derived from general systems theory helps bridge the gap. MacKenzie (1990) feels that thinking "systemically" is an effective way of "integrating individual and group levels of conceptualization" in an effort to delineate their shared beliefs.

An example of MacKenzie's idea is found in his formulation of an overview of the eight basic areas of consensus between time-limited individual and group psychotherapies. He states the following:

1. The establishment of a time limit will increase the tempo of work and encourage rapid application to outside life circumstances.
2. Careful assessment and selection is important to rule out patients at risk for harm from an active approach.
3. An explicit agreement regarding circumscribed goals should be negotiated openly with the patient.

4. The therapist should intervene actively to develop a therapeutic group climate and to maintain a working focus on the goals identified.
5. The therapist should encourage application of learning to the present, both within the group and in current outside circumstances.
6. The therapist should encourage and expect patient responsibility for initiation of therapy tasks.
7. The therapist should encourage the mobilization of outside resources that will reinforce positive changes.
8. It is anticipated that change will continue after termination as the results of therapy are applied; therefore, all problematic issues do not need to be addressed within the therapy context. (p. 17)

This digest of commonalities makes it easier to grasp the overarching foundation of many short-term group approaches, namely, that therapeutic groups that are carefully constructed and conducted offer the brief therapist even greater treatment options than those possible not only with conventional long-term individual therapy but with brief individual therapy as well.

In order to make this theory a clinical reality, the leader of the brief therapy group must be clear on several general properties that are common to most brief psychotherapy groups.

Group therapy, just like its individual therapy counterpart, is comprised of bona fide schools of thought that advocate long-term approaches and group formats with no discrete time limits.

One of the most important elements characterizing the short-term group is the homogeneous nature of the composition of the group. Members need to be matched for shared factors that will permit an accelerated group experience owing in large measure to their commonalities of symptoms, problem sets, and other factors that promote rapid member-to-member identification and quicker group cohesiveness.

McKay and Paleg (1992), who advocate a short-term group therapy model called "focal group psychotherapy," enumerate six factors that, despite differences in therapist leadership style, are common to all brief group formats. These include: a high degree of group structure; the use of specific and limited target issues; a strong and clear goal orientation; the emphasis on efficiency in therapy and the use of central or adjunctive techniques, such as the assignment of out-of-session "homework," to accomplish this goal; a liberal use of educational methods in the groups themselves, including lectures, role modeling, and other group techniques; and the discouragement of attention to transferential issues in the actual group sessions.

The focal group is seen by its advocates as a brief and concentrated therapeutic experience paralleling Klein's (1985) findings on the positive effects of short-term psychotherapy group experiences. The focal group practitioners echo and quote the sentiments of Burlingame and Fuhriman (1990), who reviewed the literature on short-term group therapy and stated that, "No other dimension reaches such consensus among the writers as does the importance of focusing treatment objectives and processes.... There is substantial agreement that a focus needs to be taken by the clients, the therapist, and the total group" (p. 105).

The focal group is used here as an example of one of many group designs that are predicated on a time-limited model. In addition to the advantages of cost-effectiveness and improved treatment outcome, the brief group model also offers a time-efficient expenditure and distribution of staff time. As a result, brief group formats are proliferating at a rapid rate. The focal group model is useful for treating a broad spectrum of psychological disorders and emotional ills in a short span of time.

Brief groups are frequently discussed from the standpoint of their numerous benefits to patients. While this is certainly the case, short-term groups offer the group leader many benefits too.

The clarity of group goals and focus counters a sense of ambiguity and vagueness often experienced by leaders of new or ongoing groups. The emotional intensity dictated by the constraints of time are mitigated by the fact that the experience is time-limited for the group leader, thereby making him/her less vulnerable to "burn out," which can come from leading one or many intensive groups with difficult patient populations over long periods of time.

Although there is an emerging literature (MacKenzie, 1990, 1994) concerning short-term groups that scientifically validates much of the clinical and anecdotal enthusiasm reported by practitioners of these techniques, there is virtually nothing in the psychotherapy literature that details the adaptations needed in order to conduct the short-term group in managed care so as to yield similar results. The goal of these groups is not merely cost-containment but also the joining of that with first rate clinical services.

In order to meet this challenge, group leaders will have to be creative in envisioning, designing, conducting, and evaluating their work in, what is for many, a new climate of managed mental health care. The brief group milieu has much to appeal to all involved with the managed care model. Employers, insurers, and payers can see the economic advantages of this treatment modality. Administrators, case managers, and others charged with the critical assignment of monitoring treatment can also reap a plentiful harvest from a type of psychotherapy that minimizes excessive and unnecessary misuse of the system. Clinicians can be trained to expand their existing knowledge and skills to include brief group therapy as another choice for their patients. Lastly, and perhaps most importantly, consumers of these services, once known as clients or patients, can avail themselves of access to sorely needed quality mental health and substance abuse treatment.

The following sections will deal with the pragmatics of implementing and attaining some of these lofty goals. The course of the managed care experience for the group therapist will be the focal point of concern. Toward this end, the subsequent chapters will trace the course of both consumer and provider from initial contact in the managed care system to the end point of the consumer's discharge from therapy in an improved clinical state.

All phases of time-limited group therapy will be presented, as we utilize group theory, group technique, and clinical vignettes in order to take the managed mental health care experience out of the shadows and into the light of a constructive and clearly defined clinical practice paradigm.

3

Overview of the Pragmatics of Brief Group Therapy in the Context of Managed Mental Health Care

All providers working under the umbrella of managed behavioral care must fulfill certain tasks and requirements before actual treatment begins and throughout its course. In group therapy, the provider has to complete these functions for each prospective group member. Despite the fact that this may seem to be a great amount of work, it really is not very different from what any competent group therapist would routinely do in evaluating prospective patients for group membership.

Managed care requires more documentation and reporting of the process, which adds a dimension not usually practiced by the majority of group leaders. This chapter will track the course of someone being referred, evaluated, and approved for group therapy under a managed mental health care system.

This process can be readily understood if it is simplified, for purposes of discussion, into six broad categories: the referral process; the precertification review; ongoing treatment evaluation or concurrent review; planning for termination of treatment; retrospective reviews; and problems that necessitate an appeal process or reevaluation of a specific case, from the vantage point of case merits and case management.

MANAGED CARE REFERRAL PROCESS

It is commonplace in managed health care systems that the patient's first encounter is with someone outside the mental health or substance abuse disciplines. In most instances, initial contact is made with a "gatekeeper," "referral line clinician," or some person employed by the managed care company to do triage and oversee authorization of benefits.

The primary care physician plays a key role in the gatekeeping process by functioning as a conduit through which people with psychiatric complaints are evaluated. In many situations, the primary care physician will approve treatment, but will undertake the management of the case on his/her own. Common instances of this phenomenon occur when patients with anxiety disorders or affective illnesses are placed on psychotropic medications, which the primary care physician prescribes and monitors.

Alternatively, the primary care physician may decide that there are clear indications for mental health care and choose to refer the patient to a mental health specialist in the mental health provider network. Primary care physicians are not the exclusive source of referral of patients for mental health services. Depending upon the structure and benefit package of any given managed mental health care group, the gatekeeping function may be supplied by one of their own designated mental health specialists.

In any case, regardless of the route of referral, there comes a point in the managed care treatment process where the provider of psychological services and the consumer of them meet for the first time. It is at this juncture that the evaluation or precertification process begins.

PRECERTIFICATION REVIEW

In order for an individual to qualify for benefits under managed care, there must be a clear and documentable foundation for why the prospective consumer is interested in treatment at this time. The provider has to evaluate the case and report the findings to the managed care organization in a way that illustrates the need for treatment and the rationale for a proposed treatment plan.

Groups such as The Committee on Managed Care of the American Psychiatric Association (1992) and Preferred Health Care (1990) have recommended a set of guidelines on utilization management that explicate the data necessary for precertification that would meet the criteria set by the majority of managed mental health care organizations. Using this model, one can elaborate on a comprehensive method of evaluating patients to determine whether or not they meet the requirements for reimbursable psychiatric treatment.

First, the question of timing has to be addressed. What causes the patient to seek treatment at this particular time? Is this the first time the patient has these problems or is it an exacerbation of an ongoing condition such as a manic-depressive disorder? Timing also takes into consideration whether or not treatment is considered urgent or not.

The question also arises as to the route of the patient's referral. Potential consumers of mental health services may be self-referred or sent by an outside agency or organization. Employee assistance programs, court mandated treatment, and referral for psychiatric evaluation by an employer are three common paths of "involuntary" as contrasted with "voluntary" or self-referral. The provider must make an educated determination concerning the precipitants in the patient's life that have caused him/her to request or require psychological intervention at this time.

Second, the issue of formal diagnosis must be addressed. Managed care companies insist on precision and clarity in case evaluation. The standard preferred by the vast majority of managed mental health organizations is the use of the *Diagnostic and Statistical Manual of Mental Disorders, Fourth Edition* (DSM-IV, 1994) published by the American Psychiatric Association.

In this system, a diagnostic evaluation is made using the multiaxial format, which assesses the current clinical syndrome with its formal diagnostic label and numerical designation. Axis II encompasses an exploration of whether or not personality disorders and developmental disorders exist. Axis III takes into account any physical conditions or disorders that may be causing or contributing to the primary problem for which the patient seeks treatment or are part of the comprehensive understanding of the patient from both medical and psychological vantage points.

Axis IV has as its focus the psychosocial stressors in the patient's life. A measure of severity of these stressors is of central interest to the managed care organization. Severity factors readily translate themselves into information that relates to the person's current level of functioning, a critical criterion for managed care assessment. The Global Assessment of Functioning (GAF) contained on Axis V tries to further define the person's functional capacity or impairment by using a standardized instrument for measuring one's adaptive level and assigning a numerical value to it. This is not only essential for precertification purposes but is conventionally used throughout ongoing treatment as an objective measure of progress or lack thereof. GAF scores help provide data relevant to the issue of success in meeting treatment goals, the need for revisions in treatment plans, and discharge readiness planning.

Prior review calls for additional data before a decision can be rendered regarding a patient's qualification for treatment. While some of this comes from a careful DSM-IV evaluation, still more information helps the managed care company with their decision and simultaneously helps the clinician refine his/her thinking in any given case. Nowhere is this premise better illustrated than with the evaluation of the patient being considered for group psychotherapy.

While DSM-IV is a widely accepted diagnostic tool, it is primarily designed to measure individual function. Since group treatment is by definition an *interpersonal* process, most individually oriented practitioners use DSM-IV exclusively and, in so doing, often do not obtain enough information that is critical to the question of whether group therapy will play a part in treatment planning. If someone is deemed suitable for group therapy, certain other variables must be taken into account in order for one to determine if he/she can participate in group in a constructive way.

Key questions related to interpersonal variables must be *added to* a strict DSM-IV–based individual diagnostic evaluation. Particular interpersonal questions that must be answered include: What is the person's ability to relate interpersonally and to tolerate confrontation by others? What is the person's capacity for empathy and identification so as to be able give as well as take from group experiences? What has the history of interpersonal function over the life span shown about his/her "spontaneous" group behavior? These questions are examples of an assessment of interpersonal function that must be made in order to make an informed decision concerning the value and possible risk of placing a patient who is undergoing the evaluation process into a therapeutic group.

As critical as this information is to the admission and evaluation process, it is relatively simple to obtain. Chapter 5, section A, will describe in detail the procedure for evaluating patients for group therapy experiences under managed care. The prior review asks the prospective provider to supply information that elucidates more of the salient clinical features upon which a treatment decision rests. Attention to the patient's past history helps put the current episode in historical perspective and includes a review of any relevant historical data such as medical illness, family history of psychiatric or medical problems, and the like, all of which have a bearing on the understanding of the patient's current complaints.

Managed care organizations require a clear and well formulated proposed treatment plan. High on the list of factors in treatment planning is the issue of individual goal-setting. Providers must give careful consideration to the question of what are reasonable and realistically attainable goals for a patient and what form of treatment over what length of time is most likely to realize these clinical goals. The more specific the terms in which the goals are stated, the more likely that the managed care assessor will approve the proposed treatment plan.

Towards this end, it behooves the provider to think and communicate about circumscribed rather than global treatment goals. For example, in a case where a patient has a serious affective disorder it is advisable to specify how the depression interferes with the conduct of daily life activities and state them as such. To say that a goal of treatment is to remove the patient's depression, while it may be literally true, is not considered a helpful way to express it for purposes of managed care.

The same case could be broken down into it's component parts and described as one in which the goals were reduction of isolation from family and social relationships, assessment of suicidal risk, start of a course of tricyclic antidepressants, trying to get the patient on a daily physical exercise program, and contacting the employer to estimate when a return to work on a part-time basis might be feasible. The presentation just noted helps ease communication between managed care employees making the decisions about reimbursement for treatment and the prospective provider of these services.

The managed care requirement of goal specificity not only helps to demystify whether or not the patient's condition meets the criteria for acceptability but simultaneously forces the clinician to think about a plan of treatment and use of community resources that will combine to reach these goals in the shortest time frame possible.

Providers are asked to present a plan for how the goals will be met and an estimate of the anticipated length of treatment. As a corollary to this, managed care companies request information that tells them about the specific methods to be used and how the patient's progress will be measured throughout the proposed therapeutic design. The intensity or level of anticipated treatment, including indications for hospitalization, crisis intervention, medical treatment, partial hospitalization programs, or whether the condition can be managed on an outpatient basis and with what frequency of visits, is essential for the provider to delineate in the precertification phase.

Lastly, a mental status examination is a core element of any initial assessment process. The mental status examination gives a vivid picture of the patient's level of function currently and helps support the rationale for the provider's proposed plan of treatment. It also serves as a baseline for treatment by providing objective clinical data that can be used to measure changes in the patient's condition as treatment progresses. As an example, a patient who is noted on the initial mental status examination to be disoriented with respect to time, place, and person can easily be tracked along these parameters as treatment evolves.

While this is far from a comprehensive review of the precertification process, it does give a glimpse into important events and a specific type of thinking process for clinicians that must take place before the first therapy session is held.

CONCURRENT REVIEW

Once a patient's condition and the provider's treatment proposal for managing it are approved, the phase of concurrent or process review of treatment begins. One definition of the function of concurrent review is that it "assesses the clinical justification of the initial authorization, the appropriateness of the treatment plan, the procedural consistency of services rendered with the measurable goals of treatment, and progress toward discharge planning" (American Psychiatric Association, Committee on Managed Care, 1992).

When treatment is under way, the provider has to monitor and periodically report significant findings to the managed care overseer. In the broadest sense, concurrent review provides a "running commentary" on the course of a patient's treatment. There are many pieces of information that form an integral part of the concurrent review process.

Perhaps the watchword for the concurrent review phase is "change." Everyone involved in the overall process, including managed care representative, provider, and consumer, is looking to see how the patient is changing in response to the initial plan of treatment authorized. In many respects, the burden of documentation is on the provider, who has to record and report a cross-sectional image of the therapeutic journey to the managed care company.

The changes of greatest concern to all are the subject of the material to follow. Concurrent review is conducted on either an inpatient or outpatient basis. Since more variables are involved in inpatient treatment, it will be the milieu used here to illustrate most of the information requested by managed care companies concerning the patient's clinical course.

One comprehensive format for assessing the clinical course is contained in the American Psychiatric Association's guidelines for inpatient utilization review. Using this model, the provider surveys 12 areas of treatment that touch upon critical elements referable to the concurrent review process. Although it is by no means the only way to conduct a formal process review, it does afford a prototype of the kinds of information that help provider and managed care representative understand what is transpiring during a patient's hospital stay.

The theme of change is echoed in the interest in specific changes in patient behavior that reflect "progress or regression." Similarly, any changes in diagnostic impression prompted by more in-depth knowledge of the patient due to the greater opportunity to observe people during a hospital stay, as compared to the brief, once-a-week outpatient contact, provides an opportunity to gain direct observational data about the patient's behavior. Specific examples of reasons for any change in diagnosis, forward movement, or retrogression must be documented by the provider.

For example, a patient who has a dramatic incident on the inpatient ward wherein he or she acts aggressively or violently towards other patients or staff serves as a specific case in point. Severe social withdrawal and isolation, attempts at self-harm, and efforts to elope from the hospital are other specific phenomena that must be reported to the managed care case representative. Goodman et al. (1992) have gone further in suggesting a system of gradation of the severity of impairment found in psychiatric patients. They recommend categorizing the degree of behavioral dysfunction along a five level continuum, which begins at level four, the most severe, where the patient is seen as imminently dangerous, and encompasses active suicidal threats or actions, active violent behavior, severely compromised reality testing, attempts to escape, and inability to care for oneself on a daily basis.

The seriousness of the patient's disability is seen as diminishing as he/she exhibits similar but milder examples of the behavior just noted. A patient at level two is described as debilitated in a fashion that precludes "independent, vocational, and community functioning and/or inhibits the effectiveness of family-social support systems in 'repairing' the impairment." What distinguishes a patient at level two from one at level one is that the latter is seen as having significant psychopathology, but it is in the realm of moderate severity and, although there may be a strong chance of recurrence without treatment, is regarded as having the potential for "repair." Level zero refers to patients whose symptoms have abated so that they no longer require psychological intervention or psychotherapy in order to function successfully.

Exponents of this system of classification emphasize that, for purposes of concurrent review, it is the severity of the symptoms rather than the number of symptoms that is most clinically relevant.

Reviewers of treatment are also interested in other aspects of the inpatient's case. Physical illness that relates to or complicates current treatment efforts should be noted. How the physiological factors articulate with the psychological factors is a helpful piece of information to report. A common example of this is found in the elderly, severely depressed person who has a history of heart disease. The clinician considering antidepressant medication has to factor in the patient's physical ability to tolerate the medication versus the potential risk attached to the decision to use alternative methods of medication in the management of the patient's serious affective illness.

A mental status examination should be conducted frequently on the inpatient service and any significant changes in the examination must be recorded. With hospitalized patients, the issues of hallucinations, delusions, suicidal ideation or intent, insight, memory, judgment, and orientation are all valuable parts of the mental status examination that help track the patient's clinical course and assist the provider and case evaluator in making determinations about continuation or restriction of benefits in a given case.

The initial treatment plan is used as the baseline against which the concurrent review is conducted. Treatment goals are regularly reviewed with an eye towards whether or not there is progress in meeting them, whether they must be reviewed as a result of observation of the patient's behavior during the current hospital stay, and whether they need to be updated or changed based on whether the initial treatment plan is or is not working effectively. Each goal is reviewed and a time factor is attached to it, giving an educated guess as to the expected length of treatment for every patient.

The concurrent review also looks at the conduct of the components of the treatment plan and tries to accurately track a patient's clinical course. Psychotherapeutic interventions are high on the list of components of the treatment plan to be assessed. Is the psychotherapy resulting in demonstrable change in the service of the initial treatment goals? If not, should it be revised, should something else be added, or should it be abandoned in light of clinical information gleaned from the patient's hospital stay?

In one specific case, a socially isolated person whose initial treatment goals included acquisition of social skills and reduction of interpersonal anxiety manifested as shyness was assigned an individual psychotherapist and placed on antianxiety medication. When the patient's clinical course was reviewed, it was noted that the patient was always late to therapy sessions. In the sessions themselves, he was observed to be self-conscious, ill-at-ease, and exhibiting frequent periods of protracted silences. He was compliant in taking his medication and reported feeling "better inside." In reviewing his participation in ward activities, the staff noted that he seemed more engaged in activity therapy experiences, was silent in community meetings, and avoided out-of-session contact with his individual therapist.

At a team meeting, it was decided that, in spite of the fact that the patient felt less anxious, there was not enough progress towards meeting the interpersonal goals of the initial treatment plan. Since his anxiety level was reduced from its initial high level, it was agreed that a trial of a supportive social skills group therapy experience might be profitably added to his treatment regimen. While he reacted initially in his characteristically peripheral posture, the sharing of the therapist with other group members lessened his authority anxiety and facilitated his entry and participation in the group. This, coupled with the group's supportive and accepting climate and its task-oriented nature—it being a skills acquisition group model rather than an uncovering, confrontational psychotherapy group—helped the patient begin to integrate himself into social interaction with others. His behavior outside of group was observed to be less avoidant and he was more available for ward activities.

Tailoring the treatment to the specific patient is a dynamic, not static, process. Evaluation of the course of that process over time is at the heart of the concurrent review process. While managed care places a strong value on time efficient treatment and cost containment, so do good clinicians. Consequently, whether mandated by an outside entity, in this instance the managed care organization, or by the clinician's own internal high standards for patient care, there is a sufficiently strong motivation to monitor the unfolding of events in therapy to insure the greatest return for the consumer of mental health services.

The involvement of family and significant others forms another regular area of inquiry in the concurrent review process. Family participation may take the form of accumulating important historical and current data when a patient is severely disturbed and cannot provide information or provides information that is likely to be unreliable at best. In order to meet the goals of the initial treatment plan, one must very often include family therapy as part of the therapeutic plan. In the case of a substance abusing adolescent whose degree of impairment necessitates hospitalization, family evaluation and family participation are essential elements of any successful approach to addiction and the problem of dual diagnosis. Family involvement helps clarify dysfunctional patterns and offers a direct means of altering family interaction, educating patient and family, and enlisting the cooperation of all towards recovery and relapse prevention.

Medication management and, particularly, changes in the use of medication become obvious parts of the review of the process of treatment. Not only is a description of the medication, dosage, and frequency essential, but perhaps even more to the point of concurrent review is the clinician's rationale for any changes in medication during the course of treatment. If a depressed patient was admitted, placed on a tricyclic antidepressant, and then switched to lithium carbonate, the reasons for this change should be documented. Was it an instance where the patient became too stimulated on the antidepressant? Did the family history reveal a strong tendency toward affective illness? Or was there new behavior noted as the depression lifted that demonstrated heretofore unseen aspects of the patient's clinical picture? If any or all of the above noted factors led the clinician into reevaluating the patient and deciding that a bipolar disorder was a more accurate diagnosis, then this helps the managed care overseer understand the basis for changes in the pharmacological aspect of the overall case management.

DISCHARGE PLANNING

Treatment under the managed care system is always conducted against the backdrop of eventual discharge planning. In the pre-certification or evaluation phase, the provider includes thoughts about discharge in deciding upon the goals of treatment once a thorough assessment of the patient has been completed. Discharge planning is a hallmark of the concurrent evaluation phase and nearly all clinical data are inspected as they relate to the ultimate goal of termination of the current therapeutic experience.

Elements of the discharge plan include assessing readiness for discharge and plans for aftercare services. The specifics of a discharge plan vary from patient to patient, but generally speaking include plans for outpatient follow-up if someone is being discharged after a hospital stay; use of community, family, and nonmedical resources to reinforce and maintain gains made in treatment; and the alerting of the patient, family, and professional staff to the risk factors or danger signals that suggest possible relapse so that early intervention can be implemented if indicated.

In the case of a substance-abusing patient, discharge planning would almost certainly include attendance at 12-step meetings on a regular basis; periodic outpatient visits to keep a current view of the patient's condition; random urine testing to document abstinence form drugs; some agreed-upon mechanism by which family members can contact members of the mental health team if they are concerned about behavior indicative of relapse; and plans for return to work or school, including a time frame consistent with the patient's current emotional and physical capabilities.

Discharge planning sometimes endeavors to get a measure of patients' impressions of their own satisfaction or lack thereof with their treatment. During this phase, providers can get a glimpse into their patients' experience of what they felt was most helpful and what factors were least helpful in getting them to the point of readiness for discharge. Group therapists who work on inpatient settings where the length of stay is time-limited know that a cardinal goal of the hospital experience is to get patients to like being in group therapy and to not be fearful of the group format. If this goal is accomplished, it is much more likely that the discharged patient will follow through with a discharge plan that recommends outpatient group therapy.

This example serves as an illustration of continuity of treatment and cost-efficiency. If the inpatient treatment plan includes group therapy, then the patient can be followed in a less time-consuming, less expensive, outpatient plan that he or she will have already experienced to some degree during the inpatient stay. Positive experience in hospital groups helps significantly lower the outpatient dropout rate following discharge. The emotional and monetary costs of not adequately preparing inpatients for outpatient group therapy after discharge often take the form of avoidable rehospitalization due to the patient's failure to attend post-discharge groups.

RETROSPECTIVE REVIEW AND PROBLEMS WITH MANAGED CARE TREATMENT

On occasion, a managed care company will conduct a retrospective review, usually by going through medical charts and records, to determine the efficacy of treatment in a particular case. There are many purposes for the review. They range from an analysis of cost-efficiency, for statistical purposes, and an evaluation of prevailing treatment methods used by a particular institution or provider to cases where there is dissatisfaction on the part of the consumer with the way in which the case was handled by the provider or, for that matter, the managed care company.

A mechanism exists through which someone who questions the handling of a case, on either an administrative or clinical level, has recourse to being heard. Common examples along these lines occur when a patient is denied benefits he/she believes he is entitled to, when a provider has a treatment plan that is rejected by the managed care company, and when a question arises about the appropriateness of mental health care rendered in a case that is ongoing or has been terminated.

Each managed care organization has its own procedure or "appeal process" that must be followed in areas of dispute and the provider or consumer must comply with these rules in order to receive a formal case review. Resolution takes place through a communication process with the managed care company and the person requesting review. However, in the managed care system, the ultimate decision-making power rests with the managed care organization.

In summary, a systematized "road map" exists that takes the provider and consumer through the managed care process from initial meeting to termination of treatment. This chapter has highlighted many of the elements of this process that affect the form and duration treatment will take. It is time now to turn attention to the clinical aspects of managed care as they apply to people who will be participating in the system as members and leaders of therapeutic groups.

Part II

Clinical Issues in Managed Care Groups

4

Practical Concerns for Leaders of Managed Care Groups

The eventual success or failure of many psychotherapy groups can often be traced back to leadership decisions made prior to the start of the group experience. In managed care systems, it is particularly important that the group leader review several key areas of group treatment prior to the initial group meeting. The central issues to be considered in this effort are: evaluating members for group therapy; pre-group screening and diagnostic issues; establishing selection criteria for short-term group therapy; and management of certain clinical, administrative, and procedural requirements essential for managed care.

EVALUATING PROSPECTIVE GROUP MEMBERS: GENERAL ISSUES

Time spent with a potential group member before the actual initial group session constitutes the pre-group phase of the managed care group experience. In this phase, the provider attempts to gather information that will be both clinically relevant and acceptable to the managed care case manager. The evaluation of a patient for brief group therapy encompasses far more than merely making an accurate DSM-IV diagnosis. In the broadest terms, the evaluation process strives to gain as complete a picture as can be obtained in a short space of time.

The evaluation in the managed care system is accelerated, but not at the expense of clinical quality or thoroughness. Ordinarily, it takes one or two meetings with a patient to form an opinion about suitability for brief group treatment and to provide an orientation to the group he/she will be joining. At the end of this time period, the provider should have enough information to satisfy his/her own clinical standards and to be able to present a coherent and comprehensive statement regarding whether or not brief group psychotherapy would be indicated for the patient just evaluated.

If it is the sentiment of the provider that the patient is a good candidate for a specific group, he/she then conveys this recommendation and the rationale for it to the managed care company for precertification review purposes. Through the group evaluation process, the provider simultaneously obtains data relevant to the decision about qualification for managed care standards and the determination to his/her own satisfaction of what aspects of the group member's life will form the basis for a treatment plan.

The more specific the provider can be concerning elements of the pre-group evaluation process, the more likely it is that a reasonable, time- and cost-efficient treatment plan will emerge. Many of the ideas from the evaluation of patients for brief individual psychotherapy can be transposed to create general guidelines for the parallel process of evaluation for brief group therapies.

One type of individual evaluation process is found in Sifneos's (1992) model for the use of short-term anxiety provoking psychotherapy (STAPP). He views the psychiatric evaluation process as having five distinct criteria: "assessing the present problems; obtaining a systematic developmental history; using the appropriate selection criteria; formulating a specific dynamic focus for the psychotherapy; and obtaining an agreement from the patient to work cooperatively with the therapist in order to resolve the emotional conflicts underlying the specific focus which is considered to be responsible for the psychological difficulties" (p. 2).

Sifneos is very specific in spelling out what he considers to be the "appropriate selection criteria" for optimum use of the STAPP technique. The STAPP selection requirements are: "1. The patient must be able to circumscribe the presenting complaints. 2. The patient must have had at least one meaningful (give-and-take, altruistic) relationship in childhood. 3. The patient must relate flexibly to the evaluator, demonstrating that he or she can experience and express both positive and negative feelings appropriately. 4. The patient must be fairly intelligent and psychologically minded enough to comprehend psychotherapeutic interactions. 5. The patient must be motivated to change and must not expect only symptom relief through psychotherapy."

If Sifneos represents the psychodynamic/psychoanalytic end of the brief individual therapy continuum, then Klerman et al.'s (1984) brief interpersonal psychotherapy for depression begins to bridge the gap between the short-term individual and group therapies. The interpersonal psychotherapeutic approach is·predicated on a set of assumptions that have at their core the belief that, as Bloom (1992) states, "Depression, as well as other forms of psychopathology, is seen as embedded in a social matrix, and Klerman and his colleagues believe that if therapists avoid that social matrix, their effectiveness will suffer" (p. 147). As a result, the patient being evaluated by the interpersonal individual therapist will experience an interview with a heavy dose of questions relating to interpersonal and interactional themes. Interpersonal role disputes, life-cycle changes and their attendant role transitions, and gaps or deficits in interpersonal behavior are more typically emphasized in Klerman's method.

Klerman et al. (1984) summarized the essential differences in styles of evaluation among brief individual therapies in the statement, "The psychodynamic therapist is concerned with object relations while the interpersonal therapist focuses on interpersonal relations. The psychodynamic therapist listens for the patient's intrapsychic wishes and conflicts; the interpersonal therapist listens for the patient's role expectations and disputes" (p. 18). Even though the interpersonal therapist recognizes the significance of interactional elements and comes closest to the group psychotherapist philosophically, still most of the short-term therapies are conducted on a one-to-one basis.

In order to make the transition from brief individual evaluation and therapy to brief evaluation and therapy in the group setting, one must not discard the wisdom contained in the recommendations of Sifneos, Davanloo, Mann, Gustafson, and other important advocates of short-term individual approaches, but rather tailor them and expand upon them to make them applicable to the group psychotherapeutic setting. Groups offer help to a broader range of patients than those necessarily narrowly defined as high-functioning by a technique such as Sifneos's and, conversely, can also be adapted to facilitate psychodynamic techniques in a shorter time frame with patients for whom these methods are indicated.

The road to obtaining the information needed to make the afore-mentioned treatment decisions comes largely from the pre-screening and diagnostic phase of the short-term group therapy process.

PRE-GROUP SCREENING AND DIAGNOSTIC ISSUES

The face-to-face interview, plus the possible inclusion of psychological testing, forms the database from which most clinicians get their initial diagnostic impressions in general clinical work. When one adds the dimensions of both managed care and group psychotherapy, the diagnostic task becomes more complex.

The issue of diagnostic evaluation in managed care formats puts greater emphasis on functional impairment, medical necessity for treatment, and signs and symptoms consistent with some generally accepted diagnostic system. DSM-IV is the most widely used instrument for arriving at a clinical diagnosis acceptable to managed care companies. In this regard, the clinician can conduct a thorough diagnostic assessment and conceptualize it in standard DSM-IV terms. However, it is preferable to present the Axis I and/or Axis II diagnoses in a form that stresses symptoms and behavioral manifestations. In so doing, the provider can amplify and individualize a specific DSM-IV diagnosis and convey it's meaning for any specific patient being considered for psychiatric treatment. The provider who does this helps to communicate more effectively to the managed care company with respect to the eventual target treatment goals and their subsequent translation into a rationale for proposed treatment objectives and strategies deemed necessary to effectuate successful treatment.

When one adds suitability for brief group psychotherapy to the list of diagnostic concerns, the provider has to actively pursue historical and current material not usually covered in traditional individual diagnostic interview formats. Groups are concerned with *interpersonal* and individual behavior. The concern for the group therapist is that conventional individual methods of evaluation, with the possible exception of Klerman's interpersonal approach, tend to concentrate primarily on the phenomenology of individual psychopathology and either ignore or pay less attention to interpersonal issues. Consequently, any comprehensive initial assessment of an individual should include some measure of past and present interpersonal strengths and weaknesses.

From a pragmatic standpoint, this information is easy to obtain in a first diagnostic interview if the clinician incorporates a group function history in his/her routine interviewing technique. In order to accomplish this, the evaluator looks at an individual's interpersonal patterns and roles in "natural" groups in their lives to date. The simplest and most expeditious way to do this is by taking of a chronological view of the patient's life, with a focus on how the patient has fared in the spontaneous group experiences of his/her life.

The starting point in this process is the earliest and perhaps most significant "natural group experience," namely, the individual's family of origin. Next, the evaluator can look at peer group relationships in childhood and adolescence. Educational experiences viewed more with an eye towards collaborative skills or competitive issues, as opposed to strict academic performance, often provide revealing insights into interpersonal strengths and weaknesses. A review of the patient's work history is invariably part of a good initial interview. For group evaluation purposes, vocational issues are explored more from the position of problems with authority, leadership skills, and other rough measures of interpersonal ability.

The capacity for forming friendships and romantic/sexual relationships is another ingredient in the group evaluation process. An estimate of essential interpersonal functions, including the capacity to identify, empathize with, and give to others can be obtained through a survey of the individual's relationship history. Critical factors such as one's tolerance for intimacy, attitudes towards power and control, trust and mistrust issues, and where a patient falls on the continuum of closeness and distance can be readily obtained if this dimension of the person's personal life is given value and appraised in the initial diagnostic interview.

Other areas of inquiry into spontaneous group function ought to include any other large or small group experiences such as military service, religious or professional affiliations, athletic participation, and the like. The review of the group history gives life to historical trends and more accurately reflects to what degree a person's current problems have interpersonal components to them.

The essential nature of understanding interpersonal style prior to placement in brief group psychotherapy is illustrated in the following case comparison. Consider the instance in which two prospective group members meet the criteria for the same DSM-IV diagnosis of Dysthymic disorder (300.4), but differ in their interpersonal styles. If one has a pattern of interpersonal avoidance, anxiety in new situations, and a capacity for developing trusting relationships once he/she comes to know people better while the other has a history of family dysfunction, trouble with authority figures, a long-standing feeling of mistrust of others, and a substance abuse history, their therapeutic fate will be easier to determine if conceptualized from a combined individual and interpersonal perspective.

The first patient might do very well in a short-term, supportive, social skills group with a cognitive/behavioral orientation. The second patient's evaluation would be apt to raise more doubts about group placement and would make the evaluator wonder about the existence of concurrent personality disorders or other associated diagnoses that would not lend themselves to successful outcome in short-term group treatment.

In addition to initial interviewing methods, there are instruments for evaluating interpersonal themes. When a therapist is considering someone for group placement it may be helpful to administer one or more tests that tap interpersonal and interactional themes. MacKenzie (1990) suggests the value of five measures that are useful where additional information will assist the decision-making process for the clinician in cases where there is diagnostic uncertainty, a paucity of historical material, or a question about the readiness of someone to join a brief therapy group at this time in his/her clinical course.

He cites the Core Conflict Relationship Theme (CCRT), the configurational analysis, the interpersonal content thematic evaluation, the life-stage developmental perspective, and the Structural Analysis of Social Behavior (SASB) as aids in the quest for relevant interpersonal information. When individual, interpersonal, and psychological test materials are combined, the provider gets a three-dimensional psychological picture of the patient and makes the critical issue of deciding whether or not placement in a short-term group is appropriate a much more precise process.

SELECTION CRITERIA FOR GROUP PSYCHOTHERAPY

In a manner that closely parallels the literature on individual psychotherapy, group therapists have concentrated on selection criteria that are primarily oriented to long-term, intensive, psychodynamically oriented group models. A representative sampling of the major writings on the subject of patient selection for group therapy reveals, as is the earlier noted case with individual, long-term therapies, valuable ideas that can be selectively culled into the formation of a workable design for brief psychotherapy groups.

The selection process consists of two central parts: establishing a standardized set of minimum capabilities a patient must possess in order to tolerate and participate in therapy groups and matching a patient deemed suitable to a group and a therapist with whom he/she is compatible. The two factors that seem to be most significant in making wise decisions about selection and referral of patients for groups are the extent of individual psychopathology and the time factors involved in the group.

Historically, a rule of thumb used stated that the more psychologically impaired patients were, the more likely they were to be excluded from brief group experiences of a psychodynamic or insight-oriented nature. For many years, the work of Yalom (1975) functioned as the "gold standard" in the field of group psychotherapy. His selection criteria are clearly applicable for only a segment of the general psychiatric patient pool. Yalom was very specific in stating that the group experiences for which he created his initial list of criteria were in the context of the outpatient, intensive, interactional group with a focus on the transactions within the group itself as they represented the intra-group version of the individual member's interpersonal pathology that he/she displayed in the world outside the group.

The other noteworthy phenomenon relative to selection of patients for psychotherapy groups of all kinds is that the literature was differentially weighted towards the side of enumerating exclusion and unsuitability criteria. This type of thinking led to potentially serious mistakes in placing patients in appropriate groups. In many instances, patients were placed in group "by default," that is, if they did not meet any of the standard exclusion criteria they were considered acceptable for group treatment. There was no consistent attempt at specificity in matching patients with groups that would best suit them. Group therapy often became the last stop on the therapeutic line for many patients, especially for difficult patients who had been unresponsive to other attempts at psychological therapy. This phenomenon of a "downward drift" into groups represents the worst method of patient selection possible.

Fortunately, this trend has been replaced by a strong effort on the part of group therapists to approach the subject of proper patient selection with a more proactive, precise, and scientifically based foundation. Greater clinical experience in working with more seriously disturbed patients in groups; efforts to understand the value of inpatient group experiences with psychotic patients; and experimentation with leadership, membership, group composition, and time variables have resulted in a contemporary set of standards that help the provider of group services and the managed care institutions with an improved and enlightened basis for understanding the guidelines for proper patient selection.

The evolution of present-day selection criteria for brief group therapy under managed care is worthwhile exploring in order to gain insight into the rationale for the range of current selection schemes presently in use. Yalom's original list (1975) of exclusion criteria read as follows: "patients are considered poor candidates for outpatient intensive group therapy if they are: brain damaged, paranoid, extremely narcissistic, hypochondriacal, suicidal, addicted to drugs or alcohol, acutely psychotic, or sociopathic" (pp. 157–158). His revised list of exclusion criteria (Yalom, 1985) looks very much the same, with no new additions and only the deletion of patients who are suicidal and those who are extremely narcissistic.

Psychodynamically oriented thinkers, including Rutan and Stone (1984), felt that five factors played an essential role in judging a candidate for insight-oriented group psychotherapy. Friedman (1989) has condensed their selection criteria as follows: They value a person's "capacity" to experience and reflect upon his or her interactions as an indicator of ego capacity; the client's ability to take on a variety of roles (for example, leader and follower); the client's capacity to acknowledge his or her need for others; the client's ability to give and receive feedback appropriately, and the client's capacity for empathy" (p. 4).

In subsequent writings, Rutan and Stone (1993) reiterated their position of enthusiasm for groups and liberalization of inclusion criteria (Rutan & Alonso, 1979) in suggesting that the "dispositional question is not so much 'Should group be considered for this patient?' but 'Are there mitigating factors against considering group therapy for this patient?'" (p. 84). Even though these authors advocate psychodynamic group therapy for a wide range of patients, they also present a thoughtful analysis of patients who are considered to be "poor risk" candidates for these groups. Their list serves as a modern-day model for exclusion criteria for patients being evaluated for a form of group psychotherapy that has ambitious goals and requires a high degree of ego strength on the part of its membership.

People deemed to be at risk for psychodynamic group psychotherapy are those who are in an acute crisis. Rutan and Stone (1993) describe crisis situations as either, "developmental crisis (such as marriage, divorce, retirement), a situational crisis (death of a loved one, physical illness), or a crisis of pathology (eruption of a psychotic process or extraordinary anxiety)" (pp. 84–85).

Other factors that preclude patient placement in psychodynamic groups include central problems in establishing object relationships. In this cluster are people with poor impulse control, sociopathic patients, chronically psychotic patients, and individuals whose psychopathology has an organic basis. A third type of patient who would be excluded from these groups is the person who has "characterological defenses of major magnitude that severely diminish interpersonal relatedness." Finally, the authors point to the group treatment contract and exclude from membership those people who "either by pathology or life circumstances" are or will be unable to comply with the terms set forth in the therapeutic contract, such as regular attendance at group sessions and other administrative or managerial requirements of all group members.

Friedman (1989) utilizes psychodynamic factors in his own selection style, but adds interpersonal criteria to his list of inclusion and exclusion criteria. The people regarded as "ideal" for ongoing group psychotherapy are those who, "define their problems in interpersonal terms; are committed to change in interpersonal behaviors; are willing to be influenced by the group; engage readily but not inappropriately in self-disclosure; and are willing to be of help to others in the group" (pp. 4–5).

Conversely, his list of exclusion factors contains two interpersonal measures: prospective patients who "give indications that they will be impervious to interpersonal influence—as in statements such as 'I don't care what anyone says' made in a context of self-absorption; and (those who) have an impaired capacity for empathy, as might be found in some individuals with personality disorders" (p. 6).

Along with the blending of individual characteristics with a psychodynamic therapeutic orientation, there has been a significant amount of thought given to selection criteria for groups that are not of the psychoanalytically oriented school of group therapy. Perhaps the most striking departure from the traditional model came when Yalom (1983) turned his attention to group work with the hospitalized psychiatric patient.

He addressed the issue of conducting groups on inpatient services where brevity of length of stay and rapid turnover in patient population were the context in which groups were conducted. Inpatient groups were characterized by being composed of very seriously impaired participants, with a shifting and unpredictable group membership, and often an emotional climate on the ward that ranged from disinterest and ignorance to overt hostility toward the idea of the brief therapy group experience.

Even under these adverse conditions, Yalom was able to identify many factors that have paved the way for proponents of time-limited group therapy to have a clearer level of awareness of what can be accomplished in a short time span and of how to select members for and compose groups that will play a critical role in the comprehensive treatment of the acutely ill psychiatric patient. When some of the inpatient principles are applied to the outpatient setting, one can see the influence of short-term hospital group work in helping to amplify and refine criteria for patient selection purposes, thereby making it available to a wider range of psychiatric patients. The seriously impaired psychiatric outpatient, as well as his/her higher functioning counterparts, now have standards by which the value of group experiences can be determined and applied in more creative and constructive ways.

Poey's (1985) work is representative of the merging of traditional patient selection criteria with essential elements of short-term group therapy. According to Poey (1985, p. 334), those patients who make the best candidates for short-term, interpretive group therapy have the "ability to verbalize a focal complaint"; possess a "significant level of psychological mindedness"; have the "urge to grow and explore"; are desirous of entering a brief therapy group; have a realistic grasp of the expectations of what the group is and what purpose it strives to serve; and have a "basic ability to relate and to be influenced by others."

Drob and Bernard (1986) conducted a 10-session, stress management group model for patients diagnosed as having genital herpes. By working in two different therapeutic modes, one cognitive/behavioral and the other psychodynamic, they helped shed light on the selection process by suggesting which patients would be likely to fare better in which of the two groups.

Piper, McCallum, and Azim (1992) extended the concept of time-limited groups to include an appreciation of homogeneity of group membership as a sine qua non of potential success in short-term group experiences. In their groups with people who had experienced major emotional reactions in response to significant interpersonal losses in their lives, Piper and his associates were able to make a convincing case for selecting patients for brief group experiences when the patient being evaluated matches the predominant group theme. Patients having difficulty with death of a close person, termination of a relationship, or other impactful interpersonal loss would be those selected for this type of short-term group therapy.

Lastly, MacKenzie (1990) has written about the time-limited group psychotherapy model and its clinical applications. He addresses the issue of patient selection and updates the ideas expressed by earlier authors by being much more specific about the kinds of patients for whom the short-term group is inadvisable. Mackenzie also discusses inclusion criteria for brief therapy groups, but his list of exclusion criteria readily highlights the progress made in the field of group psychotherapy in general and that of short-term group psychotherapy in particular in moving toward treatment plans based on solid clinical research, relevant psychological testing measures, and the interplay between sophisticated clinical experience and strong scientific rigor.

As a case in point, MacKenzie has studied short-term psychotherapy groups and has concluded that those patients for whom these groups are contraindicated are: those who cannot tolerate a high-stimulation environment; patients who, because of a state of psychosis, extreme agitation, or other reason, cannot focus on the group process; patients whose defensive styles involve a great use of projection and paranoid thinking; patients who are functioning on a relatively "primitive" psychological level manifested by defenses of splitting, projective identification, extreme denial; patients who are emotionally "closed off" in a schizoid style; and those who meet the diagnostic criteria for antisocial personality disorder.

Upon reflection about the issue of models for selection of patients for short-term group experiences, one can see the value of retaining some time-honored basic group tenets and coupling them with data from more recent research in order to maximize the therapeutic potential inherent in groups. Since time is of the essence in managed care, short-term group experiences have become a new frontier that can contribute mightily to meeting the challenges raised by the demands of the managed care format.

MANAGEMENT OF ISSUES PRIOR TO STARTING THE MANAGED CARE GROUP

Once the diagnostic phase is completed with several prospective group patients, the group leader should be left with an adequate complement of members to start a new therapy group. Prior to the advent of managed care, the next logical step in the therapeutic process would be to set a date and time for the first group meeting. Since the context of managed care brings with it a set of pre-therapy requirements, a new phase must be included before the first session can begin. The elements of this phase form the basis for the discussion that follows.

All proposed psychotherapeutic treatment plans and recommendations must be presented to the managed care company representative for further evaluation. Consumers, and consequently providers, must "apply," in a sense, to get authorization for reimbursement of the provider's recommended treatment plan. If a plan of treatment is approved, there is usually a stipulation about the number of sessions authorized before concurrent case review is considered.

The information requested by the managed care company is usually a brief case narrative conveyed by the provider to the managed care organization on standardized initial and interim treatment reports or in some cases through a telephone interview with a mental health specialist from the managed care group. In the pre-group phase, the emphasis is on present problems, ways in which personal or vocational function is influenced by the prevailing current symptomatology, and demonstration of medical or psychological necessity for the type of treatment proposed and the estimated length of the treatment.

In some instances, the managed care company will furnish the provider with a standard form that requests information about the results of the evaluation process and the provider's rationale for the form of treatment being recommended. It is in the provider's interest to convey the clinical findings and plan for treatment in straightforward language so that the managed care case evaluator can get a rapid and accurate picture of the prospective patient's current clinical picture. The watchwords of severity of functional impairment, medical necessity for treatment, and clear treatment goals are essential aspects of this phase.

When the provider is going to suggest group therapy as a part of treatment or as the preferred treatment unto itself, he/she must include the thought process leading to this conclusion. The selection criteria for inclusion and exclusion noted earlier can be very useful tools in supporting a recommendation for group psychotherapy. Many managed care representatives are very reasonable about authorizing group therapies if the provider takes care to share his/her rationale for the choice of group over other therapies at this time.

Since patients and their clinical pictures change with time and treatment, evaluations and treatment plans need to keep pace with this process and require periodic updating for the managed care company. The focus here has been on the elements involved in sensible *initial evaluation* for managed care authorization of benefits. As treatment progresses, the concurrent review process will attend to changes from the patient's original clinical picture and in the therapist's initial plan of treatment.

Once the evaluation phase concludes, the provider must begin to think about the construction of a group that will be carefully selected and thoughtfully composed in order to maximize the wide range of resources available to patients and therapists who participate in therapeutic group experiences. This process is complex and far from automatic. The next chapter will concentrate in depth on the essential ingredients in the "recipe" for successful short-term psychotherapy groups.

5

Construction of the Managed Care Group

Of the many elements that go into the construction of a psychotherapy group under the auspices of managed care, three are deserving of special attention: leadership issues, the establishment of group goals, and how the eventual composition of the group is determined. Each variable is critical to the outcome of the group experience and as such is worthy of a detailed discussion from both a theoretical and a practical vantage point.

THE ROLE OF THE LEADER/PROVIDER

Generally speaking, the group leader has to perform certain commonly agreed upon functions in order for the group to maximize its inherent therapeutic potential. As noted earlier, the leader is responsible for the pre-group screening, selection, and preparation of prospective group members. This orientation process continues on into the early stage of group development and aids in the creation of positive group norms.

The leader serves an initial role as an interpersonal anchor or transitional object around which the group can coalesce and establish a sense of group cohesion. Often, the early stance of the leader is directive and educative, while simultaneously allowing for spontaneous interactions among group participants. As a result, a group framework is established that rewards adaptive behavior consistent with the goals of the group and encourages the exploration of relationships within the group.

Leaders also fulfill a "building and maintenance" function, a major part of which consists of decisions regarding group size, the addition of new members, and the prevention of group dropouts. Research shows that groups of inadequate or overwhelming size are ineffective methods of treatment. From a practical standpoint, this means that the leader conducting an outpatient group needs a minimum of five members in order to accomplish anything resembling a productive group. The usually accepted figure of an upper limit is nine members, if the leader is working alone, and this obtains in short-term groups as well. If the leadership format is one where co-therapists conduct the group, then groups can be slightly larger since the workload is shared between two leaders rather than falling on one.

Another central leadership function of particular significance in managed care groups is the leader's ongoing role in helping to define the group's focus. The leader exercises fair and effective control over the group process in order to keep the group centered on issues relevant to the group goals and to counter trends towards group irrationality by providing a constant source of reality testing.

As the group progresses in its life, the leader can more easily concentrate on the application of specific interventions designed to effect change. Techniques will vary from leader to leader depending upon the therapist's theoretical orientation and preferred style of leadership. However, the purpose of any intervention chosen is to assist the group in reaching its' stated goals in the shortest possible time frame.

Effective group leaders are constantly aware of the stages of group development and time their interventions in a stage-specific way. For example, a leader has to be sure that a firm sense of group cohesion exists before introducing anxiety-provoking techniques. When the group is in a cohesive stage, members can support each other and can function as interpersonal buffers against excessive confrontation by the leader or other group members.

Leaders are attentive to the maintenance of group integrity and group esteem as a foundation for any successful group experience. Good group leaders have a comprehensive grounding in group theory and group dynamics regardless of their personal, technical, or theoretical preferences. Group interventions can come from many different "schools" of psychotherapeutic thought, but all useful ones put the needs of the patients and the group above issues of theoretical differences.

Certain personal qualities of the therapist help facilitate the leadership process, especially in brief groups where time is at a premium. Group leaders need to understand their own patterns of reaction and defenses employed in interpersonal situations. Since groups are notorious for the reactivation of feelings stemming from one's family of origin, the leader must appreciate the workings of his/her own original and current families in order to avoid getting trapped into problematic countertransferential encounters stimulated by interactions taking place in the group.

The leader who makes appropriate use of his/her own interpersonal style can serve a valuable role modeling function for many group members. Such leaders, provided they have a clear sense of interpersonal boundaries and limits, can make use of judicious self-disclosure in the service of effectively modeling interpersonal honesty, authenticity in relationships, and healthy examples of the constructive use of anger and confrontation. Misuses of self-disclosure are confusing and often dangerous to group members. Consequently, the leader is safest when using self-disclosure to be sure that it is voluntary and conscious on his/her part, is designed to achieve a specific purpose in concert with the group goals, and is usually less of a risk if confined to the "here-and-now" interactions in the group.

The leader who discusses his/her personal history, problems in his/her own life that are similar to those of the group members, and other details of a leader's personal life is almost always doing the group a disservice. At these times, the therapist has, in effect, abandoned the leadership role for one which is more member-like. The somewhat social atmosphere and the climate of openness in many therapeutic groups facilitates self-disclosure and the leader must guard against getting drawn into a casual and "chummy" stance, which is really a form of abdication of the leader's primary responsibility to guide and direct the group.

The therapist who is "related" to the group and is not excessively self-absorbed helps patients counter fears of aloofness and distance and plays a key role in helping to foster interaction and trust among the group membership. Group themes of power and control in relationships, interpersonal closeness and distance, trust and suspicion are all mobilized by the degree of the leader's relatedness to the group and by his/her leadership style.

Group leadership, especially in short-term groups, is traditionally active and frequently mobilizes intense affects in members in a short span of time. The leader has to have the capacity to be assertive and "take charge" when this is indicated in order to not let the group get out of hand and to make constructive use out of the powerful feelings that can be unleashed in psychotherapeutic groups. Leaders who encourage the verbalization of affect and also link it with a cognitive understanding of the basis for these feelings aid immeasurably in providing a sense of emotional and intellectual balance in group experiences.

While leaders can be active in all stages of brief group psychotherapy, they are well advised to pay particular attention to the termination phase in time-limited groups. Since the overall experience, by definition, will be brief, it condenses the entire group process over a period of time that leaves little room for conventional methods of addressing the issues frequently found to be an integral part of the ending phase of a therapy group. Group themes of separation, death, loss, reluctance to end the group, and plans for aftercare are only a few of the many termination management issues facing the group leader. The group leader has to be selective in both the timing and the focus of his/her interventions in the termination phase in order to avoid any untoward reactions or significant emotional "loose ends" remaining after the group concludes.

The setting of circumscribed goals plus the focal nature of the time-limited group experience set forth before the group began helps the leader conduct an ending to the group experience that finishes with a sense on the part of all involved of accomplishment; attainment of individual and group goals; and a clearer sense of what, if anything, needs further attention in the emotional lives of the group members.

This overview describes the general role, responsibilities, and tasks of the leader. There are many other specific aspects of leadership in time-limited groups that bear discussion at this point in order to see what modifications of conventional open-ended psychotherapy groups need to be incorporated, modified, or abandoned when the time factor in a group is limited to a fixed number of sessions.

If one examines the general principles of any accepted time-limited group model, then it becomes easier to focus the discussion of leadership in more concrete terms by posing the question of what the leader must do in constructing the group in order to satisfy the group's goals. McKay and Paleg (1992), as a case in point, state that five elements characterize a "focal group": "Focal groups tend to have a high degree of structure; have a specific and limited target issue; be strongly goal-oriented; place a high value on efficiency (homework and structured exercises designed to promote rapid change); have a high educational function; and discourage attention to transference issues" (p. ix).

How leaders go about the process of constructing a group that will meet these criteria forms the subject matter to follow.

One aspect of structure has to do with the leader's responsibility for creating and maintaining groups of consistent size so that there are enough group members present in all meetings to make it possible to reach the targeted group goals. A central leadership function connected to this endeavor is the effort to prevent premature terminations or drop-outs from occurring in the group.

There is a substantial literature (Klein, 1985; Piper, Debanne, & Bienvenu, 1982) documenting the positive correlation between low group drop-out rates, high levels of group cohesion (Marcovitz & Smith, 1983), and eventual successful outcome in group treatment. Bernard (1989) has studied the subject of dropouts and cites the figure of 35% as being the percentage of patients who leave group treatment prematurely. This alarmingly high statistic is incompatible with successful outcome in short-term group therapy. The leader can take steps to reduce this number significantly and thereby increase the chances for good results in treatment.

Bernard reviewed the literature on group dropouts and identified four categories that influence premature terminations from group psychotherapy. Leaders of managed care groups would be well advised to be familiar with this research in order to identify and take an active role in preventing avoidable premature terminations. Briefly stated, there are patient-specific factors that encompass being group deviant and not being able to make an adequate identification with the group; patients who cannot self-disclose; those who are afraid of getting worse, not better, through association with other patients (also known as the phenomenon of emotional contagion); people whose defensive structure makes participation in a group painfully uncomfortable; and those members, such as narcissistic patients, who are unable to share the leader with others.

Leader-specific influences that relate to member retention or flight include failure to adequately prepare prospective group members, errors in making assignments of patients to specific groups, and "lack of responsivity" to individual group members or to the group as a whole.

Interactive variables between patient and therapist can also be a

nidus for group dropouts. Bernard (1989) cites instances of the therapist disliking the patient, the patient not trusting the competence of the
therapist, and forms of therapist behavior that scare the patient. Examples of the latter are seen in instances of extremes of leadership
behavior. Two common manifestations of this problem are when the
therapist is too aggressive and the patient runs away from therapy or
when the leader is too passive and fails to engage the member.

The last potential source for members who choose to drop out of
therapy groups comes from elements in the group itself. Patients who
find a particular member frightening, those who feel that the subgroupings in the group do not allow room for them, and seemingly intrac-
table group issues or conflicts that demoralize or frighten members
and cause them to withdraw from group on a premature basis serve as
examples of group-specific causes for patients "de-selecting" themselves.

These risk factors for group dropouts are *not* inherent deficits in all
groups, but are best viewed as potential pitfalls that astute leadership
can counter and in so doing reduce the tendency for members to leave
group experiences that may be of enormous benefit to them. The leader
who is alert to the common reasons why people fear group and bolt in
response to their anxieties can be proactive in helping members to
stay by addressing some of the aforementioned issues that directly effect group composition and size.

Most of the literature on the data on premature termination is derived from longer-term group therapy models. Clinical experience with
time-limited groups and the emerging literature on the subject suggest
that the principles of preventing dropouts are the same for groups of
any length. Leaders of managed care groups can productively use the
information about group dropouts to serve as a guide for the early
identification of "high-risk" candidates for brief group therapy *before*
the group begins. Since there is not enough time to deal with some of
these risk factors in the ongoing group, the leader can utilize the pre-
group phase to ferret out those members who would likely be dropouts and avert that from occurring in the group itself. Short-term groups
do not enjoy the luxury of limitless time during which the leader can
deal with these problems as "resistances" or in other ways as they
emerge in the group over time.

Yalom (1975) described the two basic modes of presentation leaders
can take in their leadership posture: the so-called 'technical expert'
and the 'model setting participant.' In managed care groups, the leader

has to wear both hats. Technical expertise is exemplified in the ways in which the leader orchestrates the group experience from beginning to end. One overriding goal in any psychotherapy group is to facilitate learning, particularly experiential, interpersonal learning that comes from being a member of a therapeutic group. The leader's ability to be a role model for members aids considerably in facilitating insight and interpersonal learning. The choice of role, its timing and purpose in the group will be explicated in later clinical chapters that study the initial, middle, and end stages of the managed care group model.

Before leaving the subject of leadership, one other area of concern bears mention, particularly for those leaders for whom managed care and time-effective group psychotherapy are relatively new concepts. The issue of "mistakes" commonly made by beginning therapists in group psychotherapy is another dimension of leadership that is liable to present a problem for the leader who is starting managed care groups for the first time. Spitz, Kass, and Charles(1980) surveyed a cluster of group properties in order to determine which aspects of group work were most and which were least difficult for novice group therapists. The findings of this study are interesting to review in the light of the managed care group model. Items that were highly rated as being areas of concern for new therapists included the management of "problem patients," which encompassed complaining, help-rejecting, and monopolistic members; wanting to be liked by the group and often straying from the treatment plan in order to attain the patient's or group's favor; management of psychodynamically derived issues, most notably handling of transference and resistance; and problems in properly orienting group members before the initial session. The areas of least difficulty centered around managing confidentiality; consciously disliking the group; and administrative or managerial functions such as handling the length of sessions and arranging for medications, hospitalizations, and concrete services for patients.

Many of the areas of difficulty reflect the leader's comfort or lack thereof in shifting from the dyadic model of individual psychotherapy to a group or social systems orientation. For managed care groups, the practical consequences of these difficulties can be disastrous. For instance, when a group leader thinks primarily in individual terms in a short-term group, he/she will have trouble defining a focus for the group and keeping the group on course in the pursuit of its goals. It will also be problematic to discourage the discussion of transference issues and to provide an educational component to the group that will be of use to the entire membership. Task-oriented interventions in and out of group will be hard to design in a way which is relevant to the group as a whole. Thus, nearly all of the qualities of focal groups that McKay and Paleg (1992) described run the risk of not being realized if the group leader retains an individually oriented, long-term psychotherapeutic model in his/her thinking about and actually conducting a managed care group.

THE ESTABLISHMENT OF GROUP GOALS

Goal specificity is a hallmark of managed mental health care. Although the establishment of goals for the managed care group is actually another central leadership function, it is so critical to the success of the group that it deserves special attention on its own.

The more precise the provider can be in both planning and describing the rationale for a proposed treatment plan, the more likely the plan will be approved for reimbursement under managed care. Since groups are composed of many members, the issue of goal setting takes on added significance insofar as plans must be made for each member and for the entire group. On the group level, the leader has clinical decisions to be made that rely heavily upon determining whether a brief therapy group alone will suffice or whether group therapy will serve as part of a more comprehensive treatment program for its members. Two goals that apply to all members of managed care groups include the notion of increased patient responsibility for change and the transfer of learning of information gleaned in the group to life outside the group. In time-restricted formats, both of these factors are central to the accomplishment of goals for brief therapy groups. Adjunctive use of community support options, 12-step derived programs, and similar resources outside of the group therapy are essential in the construction of goals for managed care groups.

Each member of the group needs to have a clear and well formulated reason for being placed in a specific group at a specific point in time. Treatment has to be viewed as a process over a person's lifetime, rather than as a one-time event during which all the patient's dilemmas must be solved. Not only does this relieve the therapist from the burden of having too much to do and too little time in which to do it, but more importantly it paves the way for allowing the provider of group services to think about each group member separately and decide what would be most beneficial for that individual at this stage in his/her life cycle.

Very often, individual and group goals overlap and are entirely compatible with each other. The example of a time-limited substance abuse group serves as an illustration of this premise. The leader designs a model that addresses "individual" goals or issues, including detoxification; the adjunctive use of antidepressant medication; developing self-monitoring skills for the signs of temptation to fall back into substance-abusing patterns; the creation of alternative coping strategies to manage anxiety, depression, boredom, or other predisposing factors towards resumption of drug and/or alcohol usage; and teaching a set of problem-solving skills that allow members to engage with formerly difficult emotional issues, decision making, and other life choices.

The list of "group goals" for a short-term substance abuse prevention group does not really look that much different from the so-called individual goals just described. Overall, group goals include the establishment of peer support, enhanced reality testing for the group members through their sharing of information, and the therapist's governing function in the group. Educational goals, such as the dissemination of accurate information about aspects of substance abuse, are a mainstay of all brief therapy groups for addicted members.

The acquisition of insight and also of cognitive/behavioral skills designed to broaden the repertoire of the substance-abusing patient in helping to cope with the threat of relapse is considered to be a primary goal. Universalization and destigmatization of the concept of substance abuse so that members can feel open and accepted as part of a group of people who have struggled with similar problems in their lives forms another key portion of the group agenda. A group in which members can identify with one another and can see others having varying degrees of success and turmoil with similar life issues helps to counter a sense of despair and hopelessness with regard to the problem of drug or alcohol abuse. Lastly, brief therapy groups strive to enhance interpersonal function for all members, which is why the decision to place someone in group is often made in the first place.

The implementation of the goals set for individuals and groups forms the core of the managed care group experience. The first step in operationalizing these goals in order to make them a reality begins when the leader actually composes the group and decides which members to include.

THE COMPOSITION OF THE MANAGED CARE GROUP

The traditional wisdom in composing psychotherapy groups has been to try to achieve a balance between homogeneous and heterogeneous elements in the group. Primarily due to the abbreviated or uncertain time frame of the managed care group, most practitioners have emphasized the critical nature of composing groups in which the similarities among members constitute the cornerstone of this modality.

The obvious benefits of homogeneous group composition are evident in the observation of clinical phenomena that include a quick induction process into group, fewer feelings of isolation and of being seen as unique in a negative sense by others in the group, a clearer immediate sense of group purpose, and the more rapid emergence of group cohesion. Cohesion, as defined by Yalom (1975, 1985), refers to the intermember attraction to one another and the positive feeling toward the group as a whole. Group cohesion is not necessarily synonymous with comfort, nor is it considered a change in and of itself. Cohesion is, however, a necessary precondition for change without which the critical formative stages of the group would be adversely affected, if not destroyed.

Advocates of time-effective group therapy models have, consequently, placed a very high premium on the forces that promote group cohesion and suggest composing groups wherein members share the same problem set. Homogeneous factors can be related to psychological symptoms, age, gender, history of prior psychiatric treatment or group treatment, occupation, socioeconomic status, ethnicity, and the like.

The leader of the group in the managed care context is well advised to look for similarities among members when composing the group in order to avail the group of the above noted benefits. However, what is sometimes overlooked or underemphasized in short-term groups are the positive influences and uses of heterogeneous factors among group members.

Whether or not a group functions homogeneously or heterogeneously is largely a function of group leadership style. Leaders who emphasize sameness and "groupness," and tend to intervene at the level of the "group as a whole," promote a degree of homogeneous group function that they regard as essential to the therapeutic endeavor. The majority of time-limited groups operate in this way.

The constructive use of the ways in which members differ is an underutilized resource in brief therapy groups. Heterogeneous elements offer the ability to create a baseline tension in groups that can be used in the service of motivating the group members to change. Differences among members form the building blocks for group interaction and interpersonal curiosity, factors that accelerate the pace of the group process. MacKenzie's (1990) term, "interactional variety," captures the essence of how heterogeneous group elements also enhance the time-limited group experience.

In time-limited groups one can see many of the elements of longer term groups in "miniature." The same blend of homogeneous and heterogeneous factors found in open-ended groups can be very helpful in striking a balance in the group and affording the leader more therapeutic leverage and options. Certain themes related to individuality, separateness, and autonomy can be used in short-term managed care groups and derive directly from the differences, not the similarities, among group participants.

Member-to-member matching is the most common form of composing a therapy group. An often neglected but essential aspect of short-term group composition involves matching the therapist to the group. Once a core of group patients has been selected and the decisions regarding group placement have been made, considerable thought should be given to matching a therapist with the newly assembled group. Failure to do this can result in a group that is intelligently composed, but will fail to meet its objectives because the leader chosen for the group has a theoretical orientation, professional style, or set of therapeutic biases or blind spots, that would render him/her ineffective as the leader of a particular group. The essential point is that group composition includes the therapist as well as the patients who will be participating in the managed care group.

Once the group has been composed and an appropriate leader has been chosen, the leader's next task is to devote time to orientation and preparation of group members for the experience that awaits them.

6

Preparation of Prospective Group Members for Group Entry

The importance of the process of preparing and orienting group members for the group they are about to join cannot be emphasized enough. The group therapy literature of the recent past reflects a burgeoning interest in the prevention of group dropouts and the utilization of pre-group preparation as a vehicle for accomplishing this goal (Piper et al., 1982; Spitz, 1984) There are a variety of ways of preparing prospective group members. The continuum extends from informal discussions with individual members to structured pre-training programs (Piper & Marrache, 1981), the distribution of written orientation manuals, group orientations involving many or all members at the same time, and others.

Regardless of the form pre-group preparation may take, the leader is well advised to include an organized orientation component as a final part of the pre-group program. The group literature on patient pre-training (Piper et al., 1982) clearly suggests that realistic pre-treatment expectations on the part of patients, eventual ease of case management for group leaders, and positive therapeutic outcome for the total group are directly enhanced by pre-training efforts.

Although there is no specific data in the literature regarding the added importance of pre-group patient preparation in managed care groups, it seems obvious that in a system where concerns about length of treatment are paramount, the added value of time spent prior to starting the group has enormous advantages. It is the author's experience that pre-group preparation shows itself in an accelerated initial phase of group therapy. The theoretical underpinnings for this observation are rooted in the fact that when group members are all oriented in a standardized way, the leader has to spend less time doing this in the actual group.

Members who enter with a clear understanding of the group's mission and those who have clarity concerning the group's goals enter the group in a state of greater "readiness to work" on their target goals and are less preoccupied with issues that commonly distract, detour, or delay the onset of the therapeutic process in groups. The early sessions of time-limited managed care groups are consumed with fewer questions by members about aspects of the group that have already been covered in detail in the pre-group orientation process. Similarly, there is less of a sense of goal incompatibility, owing to both the homogeneous composition of the group and the fact that all group participants have been given a thorough briefing on the focus of the group prior to their entry into the actual group session.

Pre-group preparation should be viewed not only as a necessary orientation tool, but also as an extension of the screening and evaluation process for group therapy. In going through the different elements contained in the group orientation, the leader may discover patient attributes that were not apparent during the evaluation process and would cause the leader to reconsider a patient's suitability for placement in the proposed group. Examples of these instances will be included in this chapter as the specific elements of a typical pre-group preparation session are detailed.

Of the many options available to leaders of managed care groups, the author prefers a format that is comprehensive but not time-consuming. As a result, a pre-group preparation checklist (Table 2) is a model that affords economy of time but not at the expense of quality of service.

Despite the fact that the list will be discussed in considerable detail in this chapter, the actual time it takes to orient a patient using this system is never more than one session and frequently is closer to half a session. What follows is an orientation model that lends itself to incorporation into a time-limited managed care group treatment plan.

1. GENERAL PURPOSE AND GOALS OF THE GROUP

In keeping with the tenets of both managed care and brief group psychotherapy, the therapist has to convey a sense of focality of treat-

TABLE 2
Pre-group Preparation Checklist

1. General purpose and goals of the group
2. Group composition and size
3. Role and activity level of the leader
4. Observers, audiotaping, or videotaping of sessions
5. Physical arrangement of therapy room
6. Time period of each session; duration of the group (long-term versus time-limited)
7. Loss and addition of group members
8. Rules about attendance
9. Fees and billing procedures
10. Other coexisting treatment: drugs, hospitalization potential, other therapies (simultaneous individual therapy)
11. Contacts and/or socialization among members outside the group
12. Modifications of the group contract (e.g., individual scheduling problems)
13. Confidentiality
14. Questions and answers about group therapy (try to clarify myths, misconceptions about group and elicit early resistances to group participation)
15. Anything unique about the patient's life situation that might intrude on his/her ability to join, remain in, or participate in the group

Reprinted from Spitz & Rosecan (1987). *Cocaine abuse: New directions in treatment and research.* (p. 179). New York: Brunner/Mazel.

ment. Goals that are vague or too ambitious or global are to be avoided in favor of goals that are patient-specific. As an example, in a group for members suffering from post-traumatic stress disorder (PTSD), members can be informed that the goals of the group will be to teach members what is known about the natural course of this condition and to use the group to help members overcome the obstacles posed by PTSD that interfere with their ability to return to their work.

In so stating the goals, the provider communicates several things. First, the patient gets a sense that there will be an educational component to the group experience. Second, the target goal is not complete resolution of all life issues influenced by PTSD, but a more limited approach addressing specific roadblocks posed by the shared condition that make reentry into the workforce a problematic issue. Finally, the "message" is clearly conveyed that behavior change is the desired result. Since there are multiple roads to behavior change, the benefits derived from the group may come from cognitive/behavioral, insight-oriented dissemination of information in the group, or any combination of the above as long as the endpoint is an improved level of function for group members enabling them to resume their customary vocational activities.

2. GROUP COMPOSITION AND SIZE

The provider has to paint a psychological portrait of the group the patient will be entering so that avoidable fears that complicate group entry can be avoided. This must be done in a way that does not breach the confidentiality of other group members but still provides the incoming member with an understanding of who will be in the group and why they will be there.

Other group members are not identified by name, but the similarity of their symptoms or problems is emphasized. This reinforces the statements made about the goals of the group and helps the new member to develop a realistic preview of what kind of people he/she will be working with in the group. The process is loosely comparable to a "psychological sonogram" in which the member is given enough data to form a somewhat fuzzy but not unrealistic mental picture of the group he/she will be joining.

In the same way that expectant parents form an earlier relationship with their unborn child when they see his/her sonogram, the statements made by the leader allow the incoming group member to begin to look at the verbal rather than visual group sonogram and begin the process of group entry before the first session takes place. This expedition of the entry phase is part of what makes therapy groups of shorter term able to accomplish significant goals in a limited time frame.

In a group for people diagnosed as being depressed, the leader makes a simple statement to the incoming member about group composition. A representative example of this might be:

> You will be joining a group of people who all have been depressed, some are taking antidepressant medications, and the focus of the group will be understanding the influence of depression on family relationships and acquiring of coping skills to handle this problem more effectively. The group will be composed of men and women ranging in age from their thirties to their fifties and everyone in the group is having difficulty interacting or getting along with one or more significant members of their family.

3. ROLE AND ACTIVITY OF THE LEADER/PROVIDER

In all groups, short-term or long-term, a key source of concern for new members has to do with what part the leader will be taking in the group they are joining. Members who are used to individual psychotherapeutic techniques may be anxious about sharing the leader, puzzled about how help can come from others who themselves have significant emotional problems, and, finally, surprised by the high level of leadership activity present in the short-term therapy group.

Those who have been in group therapy before will want to know how this leader's style will be similar to or different from the style of leadership to which they are accustomed. This is particularly true in circumstances where the patient has been in traditional, long-term psychoanalytically oriented group psychotherapy. Many people who are referred for managed care groups have never been in group therapy or, perhaps, any psychotherapy before and share some of the common fears, myths, and misconceptions about what group therapy is and what role the group leader will assume.

Patients in certain diagnostic categories are usually very centered on the therapist and have concerns about how their preference for the dyadic format of time-unlimited individual psychotherapy will be served in a managed care group. The most common cases in point are patients with borderline or narcissistic personality structures who often balk at the idea of group therapy in general due to their reluctance to share the leader and the spotlight with others. On occasion, a prospective member may be judged by the leader as unable or unwilling to share in the group and becomes an illustration of the point made earlier in this chapter about using the pre-group preparation and orientation period as an extension of the group evaluation process.

In circumstances where an incoming member protests vigorously about some aspect of the orientation, it may signal the provider that this patient is not ready to participate in the group and/or may require a different form of therapy at this time. Such a member would be excluded from participation in the proposed group and his/her treatment plan would come up for review in light of these circumstances.

What the leader of the managed care group actually tells members in the orientation dialogue addresses the common patient concerns about leadership activity versus passivity; how the relationship in the short-term group is different than it is in other forms of group or individual therapy; whether the leader will be self-disclosing or not; can they see the leader outside of group, and similar "garden variety" questions, fears, and assumptions made by many people prior to beginning any group.

An example of how the managed care provider might encapsulate some of this information is contained in the following hypothetical orientation speech: "You may be concerned about what my participation in the group will be. I plan to be very active at first, in getting the group 'launched' and setting a climate in the group where people can get down to work on their problems quickly. In this group, since time is limited, I will try to keep the group on course towards its goals and I will try to make myself available to answer questions arising in the sessions. In addition, I plan to suggest certain exercises, "homework" and other things, that will require your active participation in and outside of meetings for their eventual success."

This is offered as a common model and one that allows the provider latitude in adjusting what he/she says and how it is most consistent with the provider's leadership style, and leaves room to gear it to the specific patient population involved in the managed care group.

4. OBSERVATION, AUDIOTAPING, OR VIDEOTAPING OF SESSIONS

There are settings and circumstances that may call for groups to be observed. In training centers, observation and recording of sessions are primarily for the benefit of teaching therapists a particular technique or method. There are also times when recording, especially videotaping of sessions, is used as part of the group therapy itself, as well as a vehicle for training, supervision, and "quality control" of therapeutic groups.

Observation of any kind must be handled openly and with the patient's informed consent. If a group session is being observed from behind a one-way mirror, the leader should inform the group members of this *prior to* implementing this plan and is obliged to tell the group who the observers are and what their presence is designed to accomplish. This author offers the group members the choice of going behind the mirror before the initial session if they care to see or be introduced to the professional staff doing the observation.

If videotape is being used as a therapeutic tool, its purpose and the rationale for its use has to be explained to prospective group members. Videotaping has proven to be a valuable asset in instances where the group is composed of members with eating disorders, body image distortions, public speaking anxiety, and social inhibition, as well as in other circumstances where direct observational data concerning group members' attitudes and unrealistic self-perceptions can be useful. It can also assist in behavioral rehearsal and reinforcement of adaptive behavior. By concretizing some of these issues through the use of videotape playback, the progress of therapy can be hastened by the instant reality testing that videotaping provides in many of these problem areas.

5. PHYSICAL ARRANGEMENT OF THE THERAPY ROOM

While it might seem superfluous to tell a patient where the actual session will be conducted, there are many instances where omitting this aspect of the pre-group preparation phase can be a mistake. When working with more seriously disturbed, suspicious, paranoid patients or with group members who display excessive amounts of anticipatory anxiety, a simple statement about and a short visit to the room in which the group will be meeting helps allay many fears in the minds of these patients.

During or after the visit to the therapy room, it is generally a good idea to ask the incoming group member how he or she felt about the experience. Most people will report relief, but some will describe the space in terms that are clinically revealing. After a visit to a large therapy space, one person asked about the room felt, "It seems claustrophobic to me," while another stated, "The chairs seem so close to each other; can people actually touch you in the group meeting?"

Even though it requires very little time to address the physical location and arrangement of the therapy room, it is advisable to include a brief statement about it or to visit it for the comfort and ease of entry for new members and for whatever serendipitous behavioral information it might yield.

6. TIME FACTORS IN MANAGED CARE GROUPS

Time is a consideration in any group, but is especially relevant in the managed care group. The concept of time as it relates to preparing patients for short-term therapy groups has two dimensions: the length of each group session and the duration of the group experience over time.

The traditional group therapy parallel of the 45- or 50-minute hour in individual psychotherapy is the one-hour-and-30-minute group. Variations of the time frame are common in groups with specific patient populations, varied clinical settings, and special target goals of a given group. Groups of shorter length are often employed in the inpatient milieu with a group membership that falls into the category of being at the more seriously impaired end of the spectrum of mental health and illness. Patients in this category may find it difficult or impossible to sit in a room with staff and other inpatients for the standard group session. In these instances, the group time is usually reduced to 45 minutes or one hour at most.

On occasion, the group goals dictate shorter sessions. Cognitive and behavioral therapy groups are often conducted in one-hour time blocks, but may meet more frequently each week in order to teach special techniques or for the value that repetition has in reinforcing behavioral gains made in the group. These groups are largely symptom-focused and do not necessarily require as much in-session time as they do flexibility in planning the frequency of meetings. Habit-control groups for smoking cessation and groups for weight loss are two common examples of this model.

Before leaving the subject of session length, it should be noted that sessions can also be time-extended. This trend, which was very popular with the encounter and sensitivity training group movement in the 1960s and 70s, appears to have diminished in its popularity and utility. It is likely that with the advent of greater interest in cost containment by managed care companies, insurers, and employers, the "marathon" session will become a thing of the past.

The duration of the group over time is one of the cardinal considerations in any managed care group. One trend has been to set up group therapy formats of fixed time length aimed at a very specific set of goals for the group membership. Terms or descriptions of 12-session, social skills training groups; 15-week outpatient groups for battered women; eight-session stress management group for patients with cardiac risk; and the like have formed part of our daily clinical language.

The concept underlying most of these group formats is one that tries to set up a group design that gets the most work done in the shortest realistic time frame allowable under managed care. The concept of the open-ended, long-term psychotherapy group is becoming a "dinosaur" under managed care. Groups with a limited time frame must, by definition, limit their goals. Thus, symptom specificity in selecting members, uniformity in goal setting, and deciding upon a brief time frame that allows for the accomplishment of the stated goals in a shorter rather than longer time period have become the new criteria of the managed care group.

In orienting incoming group members, the managed care provider has to devote more attention to the explanation of time factors as part of the preparation process. Patients need to have a clear understanding of the reasons for creating a group of limited length and what will be expected of them in the experience to come. A familiar example is the discussion with a prospective member who will be joining a bereavement group. The provider states the purpose of the group, the similarities among members, and the nature of the work related to grief and mourning that will be the focus of the group. In a loss group conducted along the lines of Piper et al.'s (1992) model, members are selected because they are having difficulty functioning in some central life problem owing to an inability to progress beyond their present status in their reaction to their loss. The pre-group preparation of such members helps them understand concepts of protracted or pathological grief and offers the group as a way of helping them go past their current point of adaptation to one involving greater understanding and resolution of the conflicts underlying their difficulties. Members are told that the group will be 12 weeks long and that each session will be 90 minutes in length.

7. LOSS AND ADDITION OF GROUP MEMBERS

Short-term groups differ from conventional models of group therapy with respect to the issue of whether or not new members will be joining the group. The limited time factors virtually preclude the addition of new members once the group has begun. Many managed care groups have a formal protocol for the conduct of each session and groups of this type do not allow for any changes in membership. Part of the rationale for devoting so much attention to the pre-group phase comes into play at this point. Well-prepared members are less likely to leave the group and the provider has a much more stable group nucleus with which to work. Members are told that the original group members will remain throughout the group experience and that if anyone leaves the group, he/she will not be replaced. The advantage of taking this stance is twofold, it increases the chances of having a reliable number of members required for the work of the group and it simultaneously communicates to members that they share the responsibility for determining their own therapeutic destiny.

The expressed advantages of fixed membership groups is that longer term groups often convey no sense of urgency about change, the problem of having a shifting group membership over time is averted, programmatic formats are easier to implement with all members at the same stage in their understanding of the program, the group does not have to stall or "back up" in order to orient the new member in group, the leader can focus on target goals and not be distracted by having to manage group members who are at different levels of development as a product of their entering the group at different points in time, and a host of other reasons all of which make for ease of management for the leader and greater probability of the group reaching its goals in a limited time span.

8. RULES ABOUT ATTENDANCE

All groups strive to have regular attendance as a group norm. The pressure to have all members attend all sessions is greater in the managed care group. If a member misses a session in a structured group with a session-by-session protocol, that person lags behind other members. Even though it may be naive to expect every member to attend every session, the provider must still hold this as a goal and convey it strongly to the incoming group member. In so doing, the provider makes a position statement about the seriousness and importance of the group and how vital each person is to the endeavor.

In ongoing sessions, the provider reinforces the message of regular attendance and models it by his own behavior in the group. Related issues of avoiding lateness for sessions and having members call prior to the session if they are going to be absent is also discussed with them in this phase of the pre-group orientation. Members in groups where absences and lateness are accepted tend to devalue the group experience, lose confidence in the leader whom they see as weak or inadequate, and feel like they are participating in a failure. All of these factors are, at the very least, demoralizing, but they may actually be injurious to patients who come to group with preexisting feelings of low self-esteem, a sense of personal failure, and a reasonable expectation that their lives will be enhanced, not made worse, by their joining a therapy group.

9. FEES AND BILLING PROCEDURES

The mechanism by which therapy will be paid for is gone over in the orientation session. Issues of pre-certification, proper referral procedure, and compliance with the criteria set forth by the managed care organization form the essentials of this process.

Many members are uncertain about their benefits, confused about co-payment provisions of certain plans, uninformed about how the actual process of payment for treatment is supposed to be handled, or generally intimidated by the newness of a system of managed mental health care. It is up to the provider to supply accurate information to the group member at this time. Providers should feel free to consult with the managed care organization if they are in doubt and should also encourage group members to call or write to the overseeing body to obtain answers to any of their questions.

Aside from the administrative and managerial advantages this affords, it also sets an early therapeutic tone of collaboration between leader and member born out of a mutual effort to understand and work within the confines of managed care. Specific issues such as the review and appeal processes are explained to the patient at this juncture.

10. OTHER CO-EXISTING TREATMENT

Managed care groups are often one part of an overall treatment plan for patients. The group leader has the responsibility for coordinating the treatment of each group member. In the pre-group orientation session, the provider goes over other simultaneous or potential treatment efforts and discusses how each will be handled. This category of the pre-group preparation phase encompasses several important considerations.

If the group member is also in another form of psychotherapy, most usually individual, couples, or family therapy, the provider has to get permission from the patient to contact the other therapist(s) involved in the patient's care at any point the provider deems appropriate. In this way, not only can the provider's database of information about the patient be expanded, but some potentially troublesome clinical issues, which can arise for patients being seen by more than one therapist, can be avoided or dealt with expeditiously. The classic example of this kind is the patient with borderline personality disorder who invariably uses "splitting" as a defense against anxiety. When more than one therapist sees the borderline patient, there must be an open channel of communication between therapists to guard against the patient's tendency to use splitting in the form of playing one therapist off against the other and thereby interfering with cohesive treatment.

The two other areas to be covered in the orientation concern medication management and the provisions for hospitalization of outpatients should that become necessary. If someone other than the group leader is prescribing psychotropic medications for a group member, the leader needs to be knowledgeable about the drug regimen. At the same time, the medicating provider can obtain invaluable information from the group provider referable to the patient's response to medication (or lack thereof) as demonstrated in his individual and interpersonal behavior in the group. This "two-way street" arrangement works very well in clinical instances where more than one provider is involved in the case.

If a group member has a history of prior psychiatric hospitalization or has a condition that can be unstable at times, then a plan for how, when, and by whom the patient will be hospitalized must be agreed upon. Patients who become overtly psychotic in group sessions may require admission to an inpatient facility directly from the group. In this instance, the understanding conveyed to the patient in the pre-group preparation talk is that it will be the group leader who will oversee the decision to hospitalize anyone in the group. The provider has to insure the fact that the patient understands the plan and is in accord with it in order to avoid crisis situations for which there is no contingency plan in place to address the crisis.

11. CONTACTS AND/OR SOCIALIZATION AMONG GROUP MEMBERS OUTSIDE OF THE GROUP SESSION

Conventional groups, especially those with a psychodynamic orientation, discourage or prohibit extra-group contact among members. The reasons for this group policy are well founded in the sense that the "dangers" of contact outside the session proper can lead to behavior that is counter to the goals of the group. The formation of subgroups or cliques of members that exclude other members, business or professional relationships that spring from group, and romantic/sexual relationships between members of the same psychotherapy group are a few of the countertherapeutic results that may follow extramural socialization among group members.

Interestingly enough, managed care groups benefit from subscribing to the same policy, but for different reasons. Since time is restricted in managed care groups, the group focus must be kept in the forefront of every session. The brevity of the group experience does not allow for full discussion of member-to-member contact outside the group, should it occur. This would serve as a detour away from the work of the group and in such instances the provider orients the patient to the fact that the policy in the group is for members not to get together with or have telephone contact with others in the group.

While it is tempting to make what appear to be sound clinical policy decisions concerning contacts among the members outside the group, there are always exceptions to the rule. In some selected groups, the leader may *encourage* contact among members for some reason that is consistent with the group goals. In a substance abuse group, members commonly join following a loss in their personal or professional lives. When members trying to stay sober enter group, they often have had to cut their ties to the drug-using subculture with which they were affiliated. The decision to place someone in this state into group rests, in part, on substituting the drug-free interpersonal network of the group for the "friendship" circle they have just left. These people are often depressed, socially isolated, bored, and at risk to handle these feelings maladaptively by resorting to their familiar patterns of using drugs to escape these painful affective states.

The case can be made for limited telephone or personal contact outside the group only when it's purpose is as an alternative or deterrent to substance abuse. In these instances, any contact among members is discussed openly in the following group meeting and its potential for therapeutic benefit or harm is evaluated.

Whatever the managed care provider decides is in the best interest of the group regarding contact among members, the pre-group orientation setting, not the established group, is the time and place to discuss this subject in some detail. Here again, the leader may come upon some prospective members who are unable to adhere to this portion of the therapeutic contract and may be offered alternative disposition plans that do not require adherence to the principle of no contact outside of group meetings.

12. MODIFICATIONS OF THE GROUP CONTRACT

The reason for including this category concerns the rare but important instance in which something in the patient's life could potentially be at cross-purposes with his/her effective participation in the group. In one pre-group session, a prospective member stated, almost as an afterthought, that he had a job that would require him to work at different sites periodically. When asked how this would affect his ability to attend group, he replied that he thought he would "probably miss one session each month."

While he met all the other criteria for the brief managed care group, asking him this question revealed a side of his life that automatically made him an unsuitable member for the therapy group. Even in long-term groups, most leaders would have serious misgivings about including a member with a problematic schedule. The group contract, especially in time-limited formats, should not be modified to suit the needs of any single member. While this may seem somewhat undemocratic, the problems that occur where group meeting times are changed, episodic absence is accepted, and other deviations from the standard group design agreed upon by all other members can be of such a magnitude as to threaten the viability of the entire group experience.

13. CONFIDENTIALITY

Confidentiality in managed care is identical to the concept of confidentiality in groups of a longer term nature. It is a nonnegotiable element in any group and breaches of confidentiality are grounds for immediate dismissal of a member from the group. Incoming group members are notified of the gravity of violations of the confidentiality rule and are asked whether or not they feel they can adhere to it. Obviously, patients who respond negatively are automatically excluded from joining the group.

While confidentiality is a fairly straightforward concept, it takes on added meaning in group therapy. The group leader has to educate prospective group members about the handling of information obtained in group in the member's life outside the group. There is a difference between gossip and the "transfer of learning" function in group to life outside group. Group members can be encouraged to take feedback from group to their relationships in "real life" without resorting to identifying specific group members. This is different from members who inappropriately say, as one member of a substance abuse group did to his friend, "Guess which famous rock star is in my group?"

Rules about confidentiality are restated in the initial group session with all members present and at any point where potentially sensitive material is discussed.

14. QUESTIONS AND ANSWERS

The preparation session is an ideal time to encourage patients to ask questions about any aspect of the group they are about to join. This takes place at the end of the orientation interview after the provider has sketched out a view of the key elements contained on the checklist.

The significance of allowing for a question-and-answer period can not be overlooked. On the simplest level, it affords an opportunity for the provider to get a sense of how the pre-group preparation session has gone. It also gives the group member and the leader a time to go over any areas of confusion or misunderstanding concerning the content of the session.

Since many people enter group with preconceived notions concerning what actually transpires in group session, the pre-group interview encourages the expression of doubts, fears, and irrational beliefs about the upcoming group. The provider can clarify myths and misconceptions and help ease many of the avoidable anxieties attendant to the process of being a new member of a therapy group.

In spite of the provider's attempts at reassurance and clarification, many prospective members remain uneasy, mistrustful, or worried about aspects of the group. Persistent behavior or responses that indicate a reluctance, a sense of mistrust, a fear of being attacked in group, and concerns about humiliation or public exposure and embarrassment are all clues to the leader concerning the patient's particular potential difficulty with entry into the group. In a more classical psychotherapeutic sense, another way of viewing the patient's negative responses in the preparation interview is to see them as forecasting the kinds of "resistance" that person is likely to use in the interpersonal atmosphere of the group.

Since managed care groups are short-lived, the provider actually starts the process of therapeutic intervention in the preparation session when he/she engages with some of these resistances as soon as they appear. Time does not permit the analysis of resistance as in psychodynamic groups, so that any early work that can be done by the leader in the pre-group phase reduces the need for time spent on issues that will certainly take the group away from its therapeutic path once the group is underway.

15. BARRIERS TO GROUP PARTICIPATION

The last item on the checklist is cast in the form of the question, "Is there anything unique about your life situation that might interfere with your ability to join, remain in, or participate in the entire group experience?" This catch-all question is designed to elicit any practical barriers to regular group involvement, such as job constraints, pregnancy, an illness in a family member, and other concrete factors that might arise during the course of the group and intrude upon consistent attendance at meetings.

The question is also inserted for another reason. It is vague and general enough so that prospective group members may offer valuable information not obtained in the evaluation phase or not revealed in the pre-group orientation. The most striking response to this question this author ever received was from a young woman who responded by saying, "I think your group's meeting time conflicts with my *other* group's time!" On further inquiry, it turned out that the patient was "comparison shopping" for psychotherapy and was, in fact, not only in another group, but also had an individual therapist and claimed that she saw her "guru" once a week as well.

The foregoing checklist is presented as a guide, not as dogma. There are undoubtedly additional items that other therapists would place on the list and other specific groups that would call for the inclusion of some group-specific preparation issues. Providers should feel free to develop their own group preparation and orientation formats, but never to omit this critical portion of the group experience. While this may seem self-evident, it is still surprising to see how many busy clinicians with limited time of their own either shortcut or eliminate the pre-group preparation process. Regardless of the form the procedure takes (individual interview, psychoeducational waiting list group, written orientation manuals, etc.), the orientation phase is the foundation of the managed care group experience and cannot be omitted if one is to expect any positive outcome in a brief psychotherapy group.

7

Stages of Group Development and Their Significance in the Managed Care Setting

All psychotherapeutic groups, brief or long-term, pass through definable, though intermixed, stages in their development. Information referable to the stage of a group's development is central to the selection and timing of intervention strategies employed at any point in the group experience (Spitz, 1987).

Negative results of improperly timed interventions most often take the form of premature patient departures from group. Other untoward effects, including serious psychiatric sequelae that result from ill-timed or inappropriately executed interventions, can be circumvented if the leader has an awareness of the stage of the group's life cycle and what its membership can and cannot be expected to accomplish.

In the global sense, group members struggle with the generic themes of affiliation, defining the rules for power and control, achieving intimacy, resolving issues of dependency, creating boundaries among members and between the group and the outside world, establishing a sense of differentiation and autonomy, and ultimately dealing with separation issues as dramatized by the inevitable ending of the group experience.

Knowledge of the stage of development of any group helps the provider and the patient differentiate between hazardous and "natural" developmental sequences of behavior over the course of the group. The issue of clarity of definition of phases in groups of limited length makes clear developmental stage recognition a much more difficult task. Even in open-ended psychotherapy groups, where there are no time considerations, the developmental stages often overlap and flow into one another, making clear identification a daunting prospect for the provider. Given the time-sensitive nature of the managed care group, the provider's ability to delineate and use the different phases of group development can be a formidable undertaking.

Numerous authors have described and labeled stages of group development as a therapeutic "road map" for leaders of groups. In an effort to put the awareness of group stages in context in time-effective groups, it is helpful to start with one or two typical long-term group models. By understanding the stages of groups without a time limit, one can see the processes that take place in time-limited groups in "slow motion" and thereby be informed as to how to label the parallel processes as they unfold much more rapidly in the brief format used in the managed care model.

Yalom (1985), working from an interpersonal, interactional, "here-and-now" model, described the group as having distinct stages, with associated tasks that are characteristic of each stage. In his words, "a group goes through an initial stage of orientation, characterized by a search for structure and goals, by much dependency on the leader, and by much concern about the group boundaries. Next, a group encounters a stage of conflict, as it deals with issues of interpersonal dominance. Thereafter, the group becomes increasingly concerned with intermember harmony and affection, while intermember differences are often submerged in the service of group cohesiveness. Much later, the mature work group emerges, which is characterized by high cohesiveness, considerable interpersonal and intrapersonal investigation, and full commitment to the primary task of the group and of each of the members" (pp. 299–300).

In Yalom's model these formative and working group stages are followed by a period of termination, which carries its own associated group dynamics. When one compares his model of stages of group development to one more readily recognized as an insight-oriented psychodynamic or psychoanalytically oriented group design, it is easy to see many of the areas of consensus and difference.

If the traditional psychodynamic, open-ended groups were homogenized into one prototypical model, the stages of group development might look somewhat similar to the following model. Stage one begins with a process of preaffiliation among members within which they explore issues of emerging trust and tentative commitment to the group, and are more leader-centered and less likely to interact with each other.

Stage two deals with issues of interpersonal status issues in the group. Characteristic group dynamic issues during this phase include power struggles with the leader and with other members, a high risk of dropping out of the group, the embryonic development of what will eventually become the group norms, and experimentation with competitive and aggressive behavior in the group.

When these early stages are managed well, the group progresses to a stage in which members deal with the issue of interpersonal closeness and distance. This can be a stormy stage in the life of the group as members cautiously expose their dependency longings and their sense of need for emotional nurturing. Initial self-revelation, the development of horizontal (member-to-member) and vertical (member-to-leader) transferential feelings, and the expression of intense affect are all factors at play in the stage of the group's development.

The next sequence or stage has to do with the task of differentiation among the group members. Once the sense of cohesion has been developed, group members are more comfortable and less fearful about expressing the ways in which they differ from each other. Spontaneous emotional and verbal expression, peer support, and collaborative behaviors define this stage.

The last stage of group, the termination phase, deals with the vicissitudes of separation and loss. During this period, members frequently employ denial defenses, refusing to accept the inevitable termination of the group. Similarly, patients often undergo transitory regressions to earlier behaviors in the hopes that the leader and the members will reconsider the decision to end the group in light of this newly demonstrated need for further help.

Plans for follow-up visits and directing the members' focus away from the group as the primary source of support to resources in their families, friendships, and work relationships are integral parts of the termination phase of groups. The review of gains made over the course of therapy, plus the reinforcement and consolidation of adaptive behavioral changes, is another important leadership function during this final phase.

While the definition of stages and phases varies slightly from author to author, the above-mentioned model incorporates most of the major areas of consensus among practitioners of long-term, psychodynamically oriented psychotherapy groups. At this point, it would be useful to see how some of the major exponents of brief group psychotherapy conceptualize the theme of developmental stages in time-limited groups.

MacKenzie (1990) describes a six-part system predicated on his belief that, "Developmental stages and social roles together constitute a theoretical infrastructure for organizing group phenomena" (p. 47). In his classification scheme, the short-term group deals initially with the issue of engagement of each member into the group experience. The leader knows that this phase is successfully completed when all members have "broken the ice" and participated in the early sessions of the group. In addition, members share a budding sense of inclusion in the group and a similar sense of group cohesion.

The stage of differentiation follows next and is exemplified by the recognition of differences that exist among members. Anxiety is higher in this stage and there is less of a group preoccupation with similarities among members. Part of the task of this stage is for members to acknowledge the ways in which they differ, yet to do so respectfully and to develop the ability to pool their varied resources in pursuit of the group goals.

Differentiation is followed by a third stage of individuation during which the focus is more on individual themes rather than on interpersonal issues in the group. Self-disclosure about aspects of each individual's life sets the stage for greater bonding and building of affiliative ties, taking the group on to the next stage, the development of interpersonal intimacy.

The group focus in the stage of working on intimacy in relationships shifts back to an interpersonal level in order for members to apply some of what they have learned about each other in earlier stages as the foundation for building durable and authentic relationships. The content of group sessions during this phase centers around interpersonal acceptance, rejection, and realistic expectations of others with whom the group member is significantly involved.

In groups that are working harmoniously, the stage of attaining intimacy progresses to a fifth stage, the phase of mutuality. The goal in this stage is to understand notions of reciprocity that exist in all constructive human relationships. The group discussions center on issues of trust, agreement, and interpersonal closeness and distance in truly mutual relationships.

As is the case in all groups, the stage of termination concludes the group experience. Core elements of this stage are similar to those described for long-term groups. The role of the group leader is to help manage feelings surrounding the prospect of loss and the reactivation of prior losses in the lives of the group members. Not only are feelings of sadness and depression present, but also reactions of anger and resentment at the group's early ending are not uncommon.

Piper et al. (1992) have done considerable work on the problem of adaptation to loss, using a 12-session, short-term, psychodynamically oriented group psychotherapy model as the treatment of choice. The patient population with which this team works is homogeneous for people who have sustained a major relationship loss either through illness and death or by way of the ending of a relationship, as in the instance of separation and divorce.

From this project, Piper et al. (1992) have evolved a simple way of looking at stages of group development by taking clusters of group sessions and simply dividing them into beginning, middle, and termination phases. The beginning stage lasts from sessions one through three. The task for the leader in the beginning stage is to deal with the issues related to trust, while capitalizing on the theme of loss common to all members, so as to establish a rapid sense of group cohesiveness.

Since this group model employs many of the techniques drawn from psychoanalytically oriented group psychotherapy, the group therapist also endeavors to utilize transference phenomena and intervenes by using psychodynamic interpretations and interpretations of group process as it unfolds in each session. Absenteeism from group is a common stimulus for centering the group members on reexperiencing their losses.

The middle stage of this format, consisting of the fourth through eighth sessions, is one in which the leader frustrates the dependency needs of the group membership by continuing to use interpretive interventions rather than directly gratifying some of the wishes and requests of the group. In so doing, the leader mobilizes strong affects in the group members and has to be prepared for being ignored or serving as a target for displaced anger over the experience of loss in the members' lives.

Issues may range from guilt over being a survivor to angry feelings towards the lost object. The middle stage is one in which the group therapist devotes a great deal of time and attention to trying to understand stereotypical roles taken by members in response to loss. This understanding is translated back to the group in the form of identifying common group themes that are being enacted through the various roles taken by the group participants. Dealing with one's own mortality is an expected group theme that usually emerges in the middle of the middle stage (session six).

A transition towards termination follows this session as the therapist attempts to keep the issue of loss in the forefront of the group by emphasizing the time-limited nature of the group and that it will be ending soon. Common termination-stage themes that are predictably consistent with the use of this technique are fears about the issue of changes in life, ambivalence concerning resolution of mourning being equated with the lost person ceasing to exist forever (even in memory), and anxieties connected to the prospect of losses in the future.

Group members end the final session by evaluating themselves, often with mixed emotions of sadness about the group's ending and pride in having resolved many of the issues that propelled them into psychotherapy in the first place. The therapist uses the emotions in the here-and-now interactions and makes interpretive linkages between current feelings in the group and their connection to the loss that first brought the patient to seek professional counsel.

As a final variation on the theme of stages of development in short-term psychotherapy groups, it would be worthwhile to take a brief overview of how Budman and Gurman (1988) conceptualize the salient issues. These authors work from an adult developmental perspective and the centrality of having a consistent group focus on the developmental task for each member is of paramount importance in their system. The groups are homogeneously composed with respect to life-cycle stage and similar age range for all group members. With this in mind, the authors look at the stages of group development in a six-part model: starting the group, early therapy, middle of the group, late therapy, termination, and a follow-up phase.

Actually, an essential event takes place earlier that is not included in their definition of stage one. This brief group model, conducted in the setting of a large health maintenance organization, employs a single-session, hour-and-a-half workshop composed of eight to 12 prospective group members. In point of fact, this author views the workshop as the actual first stage of their group design since it is analogous to the selection and orientation processes discussed as part of the pre-group stage as noted in Chapters 4 and 6.

This group workshop is used as an extension of the screening process, as a tool for educating patients about short-term therapy groups, and as a means for helping patients make a more informed decision about the type of therapeutic venture on which they are about to embark.

The stage known as starting the group consists of the leader making a steady effort to maintain the central group task or goal. The leader is active in doing a kind of "editing" function by his/her efforts to steer the group away from topics that are not within the defined parameters of the group goal. Here, too, as in most brief group therapy models, the emphasis is on similarities among members and clarification by the leader regarding fears expressed by anxious group participants.

The second phase, or early therapy stage, is one in which the leader tries to facilitate the discussion of how the focal problem is manifesting itself in the current life circumstances of all group members. This stage allows for reassurance and other supportive gestures on the part of the group leader. The leader's main concern is to make sure the group is beginning to "work" on its defined task.

The middle stage may be one of the most tumultuous phases in the group. The realization that there is a halfway mark in this period finds members frequently wrestling with the idea of time running out. Feelings of frustration, fear about insufficient progress, and increased demands on the leader contribute to defining this critical period in the short-term therapy group.

A growing sense of group cohesion is the result of a successfully managed middle stage and permits the group to move forward to the late therapy stage. Members feel united and are able to concentrate on doing productive work together. Again, the work is always directed to the stated group goals or tasks. What is different about this stage is that there are fewer departures from the group work and less of a threat to cohesion and the integrity of the group. At some point in the late stage, members begin to experience a growing awareness that the group is close to finishing. This ushers in the termination stage.

Termination in the HMO managed care group does not differ significantly from the same phase in other groups discussed earlier. Themes of separation and loss predominate, as they do in all groups. However, in this model, the therapist makes a decided effort to stress that therapeutic work extends beyond the formal ending of the group. A good deal of time is spent in the termination stage on the concept of patient responsibility for change, how to make constructive application of information learned in the group to situations in the future, and a review of how the focal group issue has been handled and can be handled in times to come.

Budman and Gurman are unique in being the first to devote attention to the question of what happens after the brief therapy group is over. This process is formalized by what can be considered a final stage of the brief therapy group, the follow-up plan. At the time of termination, each member is informed that he/she will be contacted by the group leader sometime between six months and one year after the conclusion of the group. The follow-up benefits both the leader and the members of the group. Leaders have an opportunity to see the results of their work over time. As Yalom (1975) originally observed, doing a follow-up meeting too close to the ending of the group is often unreliable. Members who are still in the throes of incompletely resolved feelings or transference reactions to the leader will have their objectivity clouded by these feelings.

Allowing significant time to pass protects against the problem of getting inaccurate data about the group experience, its limitations and benefits for members. The member who is still eager to please the leader is more likely to edit negative feelings about the group and to report his/her experience of the group in a fashion skewed toward the positives. The passage of more than six months and the distance from the leader and the group it provides helps greatly in allowing patients to see how the group has influenced their lives in the area of the group focal task.

Other rewards of the follow-up period include a sense of continuity of interest on the leader's part and a chance for the leader and member to review the necessity for any further treatment. Even though the follow-up meeting takes place long after formal group sessions have stopped, its therapeutic benefit should not be underestimated. It affords an opportunity for reenforcing gains made in the member's life and offers a basis of comparison, before and after treatment, for the therapist to evaluate the patient's progress.

THE SIGNIFICANCE OF GROUP STAGES
IN MANAGED CARE GROUPS

Four ostensibly different group models, two long-term and two brief therapy group formats, have been described: the interpersonal, here-

and-now method; the hypothetical, generic psychodynamic approach; the issue-specific short-term group; and the focal developmental conflict model. What is the relevance of this material for the provider of managed care groups?

The points of differentiation in the stages of a group are described as though they were separate and complete from one another, while in actuality they are overlapping and flow into each other. So, too, the seemingly disparate nature of stages of a group's life as presented by leading exponents of a diverse variety of theoretical positions may have more in common than might appear at first glance. Psychoanalytic, general systems, cognitive, and behavioral models all recognize that there are definable phases in group experiences of all kinds. The degree to which the provider of group services is alert to the recognition of what stage the group is going through is directly proportional to ease of management of the group for the provider.

When one factors in the time limits of managed care, group therapy gets condensed in an accordion-like way, leaving less time and more chance for confusion surrounding accurate identification of where the group is in its therapeutic course. Leaders of managed care groups can use phases of group development to design concrete group treatment plans with distinct therapeutic modules being introduced at times in the group when they stand the best chance of being accepted.

Knowledge of group stages gives the provider control over the group experience and prevents it from getting sidetracked on issues unrelated to the goals of the group. An example of this is found in the early stage of the group where focality of goals, preventing dropouts, and building group cohesion are the critical tasks facing the provider. The pressure of limited time is offset by the leader's understanding of predictable group behaviors during specific stages in the group. This allows for advance planning and eventual ease of management of potential pitfalls in group or threats to the group's continued existence.

Stage-specific interventions stand a better chance of working in managed care groups. The provider does not have the luxury of going back and doing "repair work" on issues that were mismanaged or overlooked earlier in the group. Once a member drops out of the group, he/she is permanently gone. The leader of the managed care group who invests time in screening, selecting, composing, and orienting group members reduces the chance of unwelcome group events or behaviors. Sabotaging efforts such as scapegoating of a member, threats to leave the group, and dysfunctional subgroupings can be prevented by the provider's efforts before the group begins and during its early and middle stages.

Furthermore, the provider has to be active in all group sessions. This activity takes different forms depending upon the stage that the group is going through at any given time. Generally speaking, the earlier the stage of the group, the more the provider is active in providing structure and focus for the group and in taking a supportive therapeutic stance. As the group progresses to the middle and latter stages, the sense of time closing in dictates that the leader be active in keeping the group on task, confronting potentially undermining efforts, trying to maintain strong group cohesion during the working group phase, and getting ready to take the group into the transition to the termination phase.

Provider activity around termination is largely designed to help the group get a sense of closure on the group experience and to be on the lookout for reactions that interfere with this goal. Members, singly or in groups, often "lobby" for extending the group time and revising the termination date. The provider has to be steadfast in keeping to the predetermined time frame and in the process has to be prepared to invite the group's anger.

Throughout all group stages, it is essential that the provider be self-reflective and alert to issues that come up for him/her in response to the stage of group development. In a brief therapy group dealing with family issues, a pair of co-therapists who had been working very well together for many years suddenly became very competitive with each other for favored status among the group members. On closer examination, it was discovered that this phenomenon emerged in session three of a 12-session group model. The content of the group session was on sibling relationships and sibling rivalry. The competitive feelings in the leaders were induced by the themes surfacing during this stage of the group.

In essence, stages of group development are an integral part of any group. They can be harder to identify in the managed care group, but are of enormous therapeutic help to the provider who has a systematized way of looking at the issue of group stages. It matters less which system the provider chooses, but rather that he/she is informed and not ignorant of this central part of all group experiences.

How the material presented in the preceding chapters can be incorporated into the "nuts and bolts" of group therapy in the context of managed care forms the content of the next four chapters. The first therapeutic encounter has taken place between consumer and provider in the pre-group phase, it is now time to move on to discuss the issues involved in conducting the initial group session under the managed care umbrella.

8

Conduct of the Initial Stage of Managed Care

One unique feature of outpatient group psychotherapy is that, in contrast to its individual counterparts, groups require the collection of many members in order to have the critical mass needed to begin the group. It is almost always the case that there is some lag time between the acceptance of the first patient for group and the screening of the last member to be included. The practical significance of this is that a patient's condition may change in the interim. For this reason, the initial treatment plan for each group member has to be reviewed by the provider to insure the fact that it is still applicable. In light of this, the provider's first step in the initial stage of starting the group is the treatment plan review, update, and revision where it is called for.

REVIEW OF THE INITIAL TREATMENT PLAN

Managed care has many criteria to be met and a preferred language for communicating information about patients' symptoms, areas and degree of impairment, and proposed therapeutic approach to these issues. Several authors advocate systems of treatment planning that make for ease of satisfying the requirements of managed care. Many of them also force the clinician to think and describe psychological phenomenology in terms that can be monitored and easily reported as therapy proceeds. The ingredients in the treatment plan shape the form and conduct of the managed care group.

Goodman et al. (1992) suggest a format that relies heavily on looking at functional impairment as the cornerstone of treatment planning.

They are careful to point out that the managed care organization is most interested in the provider's rationale for the proposed plan and how it will address the patient's current level of functioning. In response to this, they have created a behaviorally focused system predicated on the view that, "Impairments are the reasons why a patient requires treatment. They are not the reason(s) for the presence of the disorder, nor are they the disorder itself. Rather, they are observable, objectifiable manifestations that necessitate and justify care" (p. 31).

Their plan begins with a Patient Impairment Profile (using the acronym PIP) because it is their belief that thinking in the language of impairments is the best way to cast the treatment plan so that it will be satisfactory to the managed care company. Impairments meet the managed care criteria for behavior that can be objectified and quantified. Only *active* impairments go into the construction of the treatment plan and the impairments chosen as the focus of treatment are those that are expected to improve through use of the provider's therapeutic plan.

The impairment model is compatible with the DSM-IV diagnostic model and allows for recording information on all the axes of that diagnostic system. This format concludes with an overview of significant "spheres" in the patient's life that may have an influence on treatment planning. The authors conceptualize the major "spheres" in a patient's life as being the biological (genetic, biochemical) and its interplay with the patient's psychological makeup, the family, significant others, the social/interpersonal level, and impairments in the realm of achievement or reaching future goals.

Another appealing part of this model of treatment planning is that there is a provision for quantifying the degree of impairment on a four-part scale that ranges from a patient being "imminently dangerous" to the mildest level of nonpathological or absent impairments. This system helps in determining the clinical priorities in the treatment plan. Obviously, the most serious impairments, such as active suicidal behavior, a person's inability to care for himself/herself, or daily substance abuse, become the initial target foci for the treatment plan.

Once the provider has obtained clarity on the most acute behavioral components in the patient's current life circumstance, the next step in treatment planning involves a listing of the proposed interventions aimed at ameliorating the target behaviors. Proposed interventions have the greatest chance of being accepted by managed care companies if they are subdivided into discrete behaviors and accompanied by the type of intervention planned to remedy that problem. This should ideally include a brief statement about the rationale for the choice of one treatment over others. For example, if social isolation is one of the key patient impairments, it may well be the basis for the provider's recommendation of a social skills training group rather than individual psychotherapy or anxiolytic medications as an initial intervention strategy.

As Bennett (1992) has aptly noted, with respect to designing treatment plans, the guiding principles need to be thought of in terms of the plan being "problem driven," not exclusively "problem centered." In this way, the interventions chosen are in the direction of health not pathology and aim to use all the resources within and surrounding the patient for whom the plan is being designed. The unifying concept concerning the optimal intervention in managed care treatment planning is one that makes provisions in order that, "the patient should receive the least extensive, intensive, intrusive and costly intervention capable of successfully addressing the present problem" (p. 207). Outcome objectives are another key element in any acceptable managed care treatment plan. They will play an increasingly important role as therapy progresses in evaluating the effectiveness of treatment and the authorization or denial of payment for further services. A detailed discussion of outcome measures will be reviewed in Chapter 13. In terms of treatment planning, a comprehensive treatment plan should include a look toward the future, with some projection by the provider about anticipated results within a reasonable time frame.

The increased presence of managed care programs of different kinds has brought with it a slew of prototypes for the design of a treatment plan. Managed care organizations themselves have issued preferred standards for treatment planning, as have independent clinicians and administrators. This can make for confusion among providers regarding the choice of treatment plan that will be acceptable to the organization responsible for reviewing the provider's proposed approach to treatment.

When dealing with managed care companies that have their own formal guidelines, the provider is well advised to report the treatment plan in the terminology used in the provider manuals supplied by the managed care company. When no such specific guidelines are available, the provider can simplify the process of creating and reporting the treatment plan by thinking in terms of general properties of treatment planning that contain the essential elements that nearly any managed care organization would consider as reasonable.

Thinking more in general terms about constructing a managed care treatment approach allows providers some latitude to express their thoughts in a less regimented way as long as they address the major aspects of the essentials of initial treatment planning. Bennett (1992) has identified three broad aspects of treatment planning that serve as an example of the above. In his system, the provider is obligated to include three areas of the patient's life as a means of covering the majority of the essential information required for the initial treatment plan report. Very simply, the first segment comments on the presenting problem and how it adversely intrudes into the patient's life either in the form of specific symptoms or in an inability to progress in key areas of function due to the presenting problem. A brief review of the patient's relevant past history referable to the presenting complaint can also be included here.

The second broad area of focus in treatment identifies "limiting factors" in the patient and his/her current life circumstances. This is the point at which the provider submits information comparable to the "level of impairment" paradigm in the PIP system noted earlier in this section. This is the section of the treatment plan involving the decision about the degree of urgency of treatment and the level of care (i.e., hospitalization, day treatment, outpatient, etc.) that most effectively attends to the presenting symptoms.

The third overall category in this plan is directed at what the personal, social, and occupational resources are and the patient's current capacity for gaining access to them in a way that can be used as source of benefit in planning overall treatment.

Regardless of the specific format used and method of reporting chosen by any given provider, the endpoint of a successful treatment plan, aside from gaining approval from the managed care evaluators, is, as Bennett states, "The establishment of a helping relationship, and second, agreement on objectives for the intervention and on the focus necessary to achieve them. The choice of methodology, which is essentially a strategic decision, follows from a consideration of the resources available, a judgment about how the patient is likely to work best, and a frank discussion with the patient" (p. 209).

Whether the provider chooses a specific managed care program's set of guidelines or prefers the use of the more open model just noted, it is clear that managed care looks for information that is clearly stated, is associated with the present condition for which treatment is being proposed, reviews the assets and limitations in the patient's current life, and provides a formula for intervention with a sensible rationale for the inclusion of each element of the recommended therapeutic approach.

With the philosophy of treatment planning described above, it is timely to explore how a treatment plan that features brief group psychotherapy as its centerpiece might look in an actual case example. Due to the nature of the fact that groups consist of minimally six to eight members, it would be impractical to review here a model treatment plan for every group member. In the actual clinical setting, the provider actually does review each patient's treatment plan and current clinical status before starting the first group session.

In an effort to cover more material in less time, the case chosen for illustration of treatment planning is one where the patient has a dual diagnosis of substance abuse and an affective disorder. By presenting the material in this way, we will afford the option of "condensing two cases into one," allowing for the discussion of treatment planning for two distinct conditions. Another reason for choosing to present the material in this way is that this more closely approximates the task for the provider starting the group, who must conduct several simultaneous case reviews in order to cover all the participants in the group.

A MODEL TREATMENT PLAN FOR A
SPECIFIC MANAGED CARE GROUP MEMBER

Case History

John X. is a 25-year-old, divorced, unemployed automobile mechanic with a medical history of thyroid disease. He came to the emergency room of a general hospital in an intoxicated state. When asked what precipitated this episode, he stated that his girlfriend had left him for another man and he was "feeling real depressed."

He acknowledges a long-standing history of experimentation with alcohol and marijuana starting when he was a high school sophomore.

He has a history of academic difficulty and poor school performance. He describes himself as a "loner" with no close friends or family ties.

His family history reveals a parental divorce when the patient was five years old. His verbally abusive, alcoholic father abandoned the family, leaving John and his younger brother to live with their mother. John's mother is described as hardworking, "serious," and "down in the dumps a lot." As a result of his mother's need to work in order to support the family, a lot of John's time during his younger years was spent with his maternal grandmother, a "kind and loving woman" who died six months ago.

John's work history is spotty due to his episodic substance use, but when employed he describes "loving my work" and liking to do "something I'm good at." The longest period of uninterrupted employment was a two-year period during which he established some superficial relationships with co-workers and used only moderate amounts of alcohol when "I went out with the guys for a beer after work." He takes pride in being "good with my hands" and feels a sense of accomplishment when he does car repairs or works on customizing and restoring antique automobiles, a hobby he has pursued regularly since his high school days.

Target Elements in the Treatment Plan

Two areas of concern are apparent in the case history: depression and substance abuse. The initial focus of the managed care plan is on the events surrounding his arrival at the hospital in an intoxicated state. Step one of the treatment plan would be to inquire further into these two target areas. In so doing, the provider would note that the issues of loss and isolation have been problematic for John to handle and that he connected his intensified use of drugs to the break-up with his girlfriend, but really had resumed heavier substance use following his grandmother's death.

The results of urine toxicology testing at the time of his emergency visit revealed evidence of current cocaine use. The provider, given the information in the case, should be thinking along several lines in the construction of the treatment plan for John. First on the list of concerns would be the assessment of his depression and his potential for suicidal or self-destructive behavior. Closely allied to this has to be some further determination and assessment of the extent, type, and severity of his drug use. Information referable to suicidality and degree of severity of substance abuse is used to decide where the most appropriate setting for the patient would be. Is hospitalization necessary or can he be managed on an outpatient basis? The answers to these questions are also reflected in the selection of immediate target goals for the patient.

If one assumes that some basic information, including a formal mental status examination, has been done by the provider or the emergency room staff, then certain information will be available that is critical to initial decision making in the case. In John's case, he is seen in the ER, stays overnight, and is lucid enough in the morning to be interviewed by a provider who is assessing his need for treatment.

The results of the interview are as follows:

1. John's mental status exam reveals a shallow affect and fleeting suicidal ideation, but he denies any concrete plan or intent with respect to self-harm.
2. It appears that John considers himself a "recreational" drug user and his current drugs of choice are alcohol and cocaine. He uses beer on a daily basis and "snorts" cocaine "when I can afford to buy it or when friends offer it to me." He has never used "crack" nor has he used "free-base" cocaine.
3. There is no evidence of formal thought disorder or evidence of psychosis on his mental status exam and throughout the course of the interview he relates in an appropriate manner.
4. His demeanor is noted to be shy and interpersonally avoidant, although he is cooperative with the evaluator.
5. John states that, "I really think I need help."
6. John presents the following neurovegetative signs of depression: sleep disturbance (hypersomnia), excessive interest in food (with weight gain of 20 pounds in the past three months), diminished concentration span, a regular sense of being "unhappy" most of the time, an absence of sexual desire, and a general feeling of "sluggishness."

In looking ahead toward treatment planning, the provider should be thinking in specific diagnostic terms, formulating a sense of the areas of John's assets and liabilities, and keeping an eye fixed on the future concerning what some useful long-term goals might be for a young man who presents the aforementioned clinical behaviors and symptoms.

Initial Treatment Plan

The decision is made to recommend outpatient treatment for John. His level of impairment is level one, moderate, using the PIP severity of impairment scale in which zero reflects no pathological impairment and four, the highest, denotes imminently dangerous behaviors.

Given all the above information, John's treatment plan might look as follows:

Presenting Problems

1. Dysphoric mood.
2. Substance abuse, alcohol and cocaine.
3. Social isolation.

DSM-IV Diagnosis

Axis I
Major depression, single episode–296.2
Alcohol intoxication/abuse–305.0
Cocaine abuse–305.60

Axis II
Avoidant personality disorder–301.82 (Rule out)

Axis III
Thyroid dysfunction: Hypothyroidism

Axis IV
Severity of psychosocial stressors: Moderate

Axis V
Global Assessment of Functioning Score: 65

FUNCTIONAL IMPAIRMENTS

1. Currently unable to hold a job on a consistent basis.
2. Interpersonal relationship dysfunction (estranged from family; recent breakup of romantic relationship).
3. Inadequate health care skills in managing his medication for hypothyroidism.
4. Active alcohol and cocaine use, which contributes to absenteeism and interpersonal conflicts in his work.

TARGET GOALS

1. Detoxification from drugs of abuse. Since his alcohol and cocaine consumption are of a moderate level (no "blackouts," seizures, or other withdrawal symptoms), this can be done on an outpatient basis.
2. Assess the state of the patient's current medical status.
3. Evaluate the patient for the concurrent use of antidepressant medication.
4. Review the patient's past history in greater depth, looking for past psychiatric, drug, or medical treatment episodes.
5. Assess the patient's motivation for treatment of his substance abuse problems and his depressive symptoms.

PROPOSED INTERVENTIONS

1. Have the patient come in three times per week for the first two weeks for purposes of monitoring sobriety. These visits will be 30 minutes or less, after which the patient will leave a urine sample for drug testing.
2. Perform a complete physical examination and order appropriate blood and urine tests. Look for the state of stability of the patient's thyroid medication management, rule out other concomitant physical illness that might simulate depression. Check to make sure there is no evidence of other endocrinological disease, HIV, and/or hepatitis.
3. Perform a psychopharmacological evaluation for tricyclic or SSRI antidepressant medication.

4. Obtain the patient's past hospital records.
5. Evaluate the patient for placement in a time-limited psychotherapy group.

ESTIMATE OF ASSETS IN THE PATIENT'S LIFE

1. Presence of positive desire to give up alcohol and cocaine use.
2. Ability to sustain interest in projects over time (his interest in antique car restoration).
3. Possible linkages with younger brother and mother for family involvement in patient's drug rehabilitation plan.
4. No history of prior failure in any drug treatment program.
5. Has never had a trial of antidepressant medication.
6. Positive relationship with maternal grandmother.

The results of the initial treatment plan are that John is found to be medically sound and only needs to take thyroid medication once daily; he keeps his first two weeks of outpatient appointments and has no laboratory evidence of active drug use; a review of his prior hospital records is unremarkable; and he is deemed suitable for entry into a short-term, men's substance-abuse group. During this period, John was placed on the tricyclic antidepressant desipramine and is currently taking 100 mg. per day.

Entry Into the Group: The First Group Session

The initial treatment plan has been in effect and that portion of the plan focusing on John's participation in a managed care group forms the essence of the material to be presented. This is done with the understanding that other elements help comprise the totality of John's treatment plan over the course of time. As we trace the life of the group and John's role in it, significant aspects of other treatment, psychological testing, family, phenomenological, medication, and psychotherapeutic elements will be highlighted.

This treatment plan revolves around the use of group as the "hub of the wheel" in the overall treatment plan. Group will also be involved in another way when the provider recommends simultaneous membership in a self-help group based on the 12-step model of Alcoholics Anonymous as another requirement of John's effort to be abstinent from drugs of abuse.

Once the provider has gone through a review, and possible revision, of the treatment plans of all the group members, the group is ready to begin. Step one has to be the process of facilitating entry into group for all participants. In order to accomplish this, the provider has to anticipate many factors, from the mundane to the profound, that influence group entry. The easiest way to see this process in action is to look at aspects of a typical initial session in a managed care group.

One advantage the provider has in starting the group is the return on the investment in time spent preparing all group members in the pre-group phase. Group preparation is standardized for all incoming members and, correspondingly, all members can be expected to be knowledgeable about the group, its goals, why they were chosen for this particular group, and how the leader plans to be involved in the group process.

The homogeneous group composition helps facilitate entry because patients can immediately see aspects of themselves reflected in others in the group. Not only does this contribute to getting the group off to a fast start, it lessens the tension connected to perceptions of goal incompatibility among members, which, in turn, lessens the likelihood of group members dropping out prematurely.

Of the varied tasks the provider has to carry out in the first session, some may seem more administrative or managerial while others look more recognizably "therapeutic." It is safe to assume that all early therapist behavior in the group, as well as the way in which the leader structures the group experience, is watched carefully by the membership. Even the most extensive pre-group preparation does not obliterate the apprehension members share about joining the new group, it merely reduces anxiety to tolerable levels so that incoming patients can be free enough of their worries to begin to participate actively in the initial meetings of the group.

The leader/provider is responsible for many functions in the first session. Once a full group membership is in place, a starting date and time are conveyed to the members. At some point prior to the first meeting, the provider has to find a suitable space to hold the sessions. Ideally, a room with freely movable chairs allows the leader to see how members seat themselves spontaneously and how their physical arrangement in space may be reflective of dynamic issues in the group. Common examples are the member who designates one chair as "my regular seat," the member who feels most comfortable sitting nearest the leader, and the members who choose to sit "together" all the time. These are all pieces of data that give clues as to how different group members handle their initial anxieties in new interpersonal experiences.

The leader is well advised to seat himself last, allowing room for some of the above noted behavior to take place. Some leaders like to have more chairs than members so that in groups where physical closeness may be unbearable, as is the case with patients with paranoid traits, members have increased options and control over interpersonal closeness and distance.

Most managed care groups begin with the provider taking the lead in modeling several things that will ultimately be woven into the fabric of the group as positive norms. First, the leader starts the group on time and facilitates the introduction of members to one another. One thing unique to the managed care group is that the leader checks with all the members to be sure that their "paperwork" is in order and that they are aware of what the particular managed care system requires on their part for continued authorization of treatment benefits. Any confusion surrounding the "mechanics" of managed care is handled by the leader before the session starts. Questions are answered directly and are not to be treated as "resistances." The managed care system is new to many members who may, quite appropriately, rely on the leader as their source for accurate direction and information.

As in a chess match, there are some standard "opening moves" that come originally from longer term group models but work equally well in brief therapy groups. One such instance can be seen in the method by which the leader starts the session after everyone has been introduced. The leader begins with an opening set of remarks that are basically a review and restatement of the pre-group orientation given to each member prior to the start of the group. The group goals, time frame, and some underscoring of the critical nature of confidentiality in groups is emphasized in the provider's opening remarks.

The leader also makes a point of stating the group's "ground rules" with all members present. Doing this at the first session avoids the subsequent problem of members deviating from the group goals and rationalizing or justifying their behavior by claiming that the therapist never told them that certain intra- or extra-group activities or behaviors were prohibited.

In the time-limited, managed care substance abuse group, which John has just joined, the leader would voice the following set of group standards: (1) The goal of the group is to help oneself and others abstain from drug and alcohol use. (2) Each member must be prepared to be totally honest about current and historical drug use. (3) An absolute commitment is made to refrain from using any mind or mood-altering substances. (4) Regular attendance is mandatory and excessive absences are destructive to the group and its mission. (5) No one may come to the group while actively under the influence of drugs or alcohol. (6) "Slips," i.e., using drugs during the course of the group, will be initially treated as potential learning experiences. However, repeated slips are self-defeating and may require treatment other than short-term group therapy such as hospitalization. (7) All group members agree to have random urine testing for the presence of drugs done at the discretion of the leader. (8) Members are asked not to socialize with each other outside of the group. (9) The group leader has the permission of each member to be in contact with family members or with any other therapists who may be involved in his/her care. (10) Absolute confidentiality is a nonnegotiable core element of the group. Violations of the confidentiality agreement are grounds for immediate dismissal from group.

The leader/provider does a number of other things in the first session that are designed primarily to foster group interaction. By emphasizing similarities among members, modeling a posture of intellectual honesty, taking a supportive stance, and encouraging the expression of genuine affect, the leader contributes to the creation of a group atmosphere in which suspiciousness, fear, and hostility are replaced by mutual respect, collaboration, and strong positive identifications with other members and with the group leader.

It is wise for the group provider to be on the alert for common first-session themes and characteristic group roles taken by the different "players" in the group. One universal group theme expressed in the early sessions relates to issues of inclusion and exclusion of members. Patients are concerned about their place in the group hierarchy and whether or not they will be accepted by others. In some sense, the inclusion/exclusion dimension closely parallels another frequent early group issue, the establishment of trust in relationships.

An unspoken question on the minds of many in the group is whether they can be themselves and be assured that no harm will come to them. Since many people who join groups have not had good experiences in their original families or other significant interpersonal venues, there is a fear about the risk of self-disclosure and its imagined consequences. The leader has to be active in identifying these issues as fears and delineating how this group will function as a "corrective emotional experience" for the participants. In short-term groups, the leader accomplishes this by keeping a relentless focus on the group goals and actively interrupting any potential for interpersonal damage in the group.

The other central area of group concern in the initial and early sessions addresses aspects of dependency needs on the part of various group members. Characteristic early group behavior typifying this phenomenon can be found in the member who consistently tries to engage in dialogues with the leader to the point of ignoring others in the room. This denial of "groupness" and tenacity in trying to maintain a dyadic relationship with the leader, despite the presence of seven or eight other members, is best viewed as a desperate attempt to negotiate what is experienced as a potentially overwhelming interpersonal event for the member in question.

Some members with either unresolved dependency issues and/or power and control issues go another route and devalue the importance of the leader. Counterdependent postures taken by members who try to convince others that the leader is superfluous, inadequate, insensitive, too active, too passive, or some other demeaning characterization are often voicing their own fears about negative consequences resulting from misuses of the therapist's perceived power in the group.

"Testing" the leader is a final manifestation of initial membership anxiety about the group they are joining. The "message" to the leader is something in the nature of, "Are you competent, strong, experienced, enough to be relied upon to take good care of the group?" Leadership challenges in the early phase of managed care groups are best seen as indirect requests for reassurance. The leader who mistakenly enters into a power struggle with a challenging or testing member usually "fails the test" and gets embroiled in an avoidable power struggle with a fearful patient.

In managed care groups, the limit in the number of sessions often scares the group members, many of whom cannot imagine how the leader is going to help them accomplish their treatment goals in such a minuscule time frame. By constantly keeping the group on task, giving direction when needed, and performing an educational function, the leader can use leadership activities to show the group that positive change is indeed possible within the given time limits.

Managed care groups may also be locales in which a variety of early session behaviors are previews of the varied ways in which members try to cope with their fears about being in groups. Prolonged silences; superficial social chatter; premature self- disclosure, in which a member "tells too much too soon" or cannot effectively edit his/her thoughts; members who avoid anxiety in group situations by excessive talking or by monopolizing the group time; and those who take an argumentative or oppositional stance, are all telling the leader something valuable through their actions. In many groups, part of the group's target goal is to identify these familiar but inflexible roles taken by members and supply more adaptive alternative ways of interacting when one feels anxious in group or social situations.

Group providers should observe nonverbal communications in the early group sessions as another valuable channel for information about the positive and negative feelings being generated between members and towards the therapist. As the group progresses, the leader may find this a useful dimension to facilitate the implementation of the goals for certain group members who routinely have trouble translating their feelings into words. The initial managed care group session usually ends with a closing statement or summary by the leader. This is done in a first meeting in order to pick out and reward the statements and behaviors that are most consonant with the purpose of the group. A closing statement reinforces the leader's role as governor of the group experience and lends a sense of clear closure to the session.

Some leaders of brief therapy groups prefer to leave some time for questions by members before making their closing comments. Those who prefer this way of concluding an initial or early meeting see it as advantageous to use the question and answer period as a rough measure of how the group is reacting to each session. The feedback that the group members provide by the content and focus of their questions is used in planning subsequent sessions and future interventions.

A variation on this ending is to allow time before the first session ends to have a group "go-around" wherein each member voices his/her reaction to the initial session. Some leaders view this as essential in helping the leader gauge the impact of the first session on all members.

A frequent response in a first-session go-around is one of relief over the fact that many of the member's preconceived fears about the group did not come to pass. Many leaders recognize the powerful influence of consensual validation by peers in building group cohesion and use the final few minutes to give members a chance to respond to the question, "How did you feel about this first session?"

Finally, the leader makes sure to end on time, once again illustrating the finite nature of each session and of the limits on therapy imposed by time constraints. The leader also is the one who makes the final statement in the group as a way of demonstrating his/her ability to set appropriate limits in the group, a leadership quality that is extremely comforting to those members who are worried about emotions or impulses getting out of control in group meetings.

Once the first session is completed, the managed care group is underway and the leader can begin to focus less on an introductory role and more on his or her ability to build a therapeutic alliance with the group in order to help implement change in the group. How this process develops in the time-limited managed care group forms the subject matter for a discussion of the middle stage of managed care groups.

9

The Middle Stage of Brief Groups: Problems and Solutions

The middle stage of managed care groups is equivalent to the working through phase of conventional groups, during which insights, in psychodynamically oriented groups, and cognitive or behavioral principles, in groups of a more symptom-oriented nature, are put into action or applied in the patient's life. It is also the stage in which ambivalent feelings about change are most prominent.

Certainly, in long-term groups, the middle stage is the longest phase and in many ways the most difficult stage to explicate in the short-term milieu. One useful way to approach the topic is to view the middle stage as one that presents many opportunities for change and growth along with strong forces pulling in the direction of sameness and inflexibility. The provider can simplify the potentially confusing events and actions that exemplify the middle phase of brief group therapy by conceptualizing certain commonly occurring situations that could present barriers to the group's progress.

TIME FACTORS

One inevitable aspect of the middle stage of managed care groups is the growing awareness for the provider and the patient alike that the group is moving closer to its endpoint. The denial of the ending of the group and the sense of security emanating from a firm sense of group cohesiveness that characterize earlier stages of the group begin to compete with contrasting emotions that stem from the knowledge that with each passing session, the group is nearing its time limit. This frequently creates a sense of urgency and anxiety in group members that can be used to therapeutic advantage.

The sense that time is running out and that there are still issues to be resolved can be a motivating factor for the group membership. The group often feels frustrated, frightened, and angry. Any or all of these feelings can be directed towards the leader, who the group feels may have disappointed them. At times, the amalgamation of emotions can reach near crisis proportions, which poses a threat to the viability of the group itself. The attitude of ongoing ambivalence about change on the members' part complicates the work of the group and calls for astute leadership and therapeutic skill in order to avert a potential group disaster.

The leader can capitalize on the peer support elements to help members learn to reach out to contemporaries, rather than to the parental figure personified by the therapist, in order to cope with trying emotional times. This is a critical time for the provider to keep the group focused on its goals. Since there are such strong emotional forces at play in the middle stage of brief groups, the group runs the risk of getting detoured onto other topics that are not part of the original group contract.

EMOTIONAL INTENSITY OF THE MIDDLE STAGE

A favorable by-product of the highly charged group atmosphere of the middle stage is the opportunity for the experiential learning that can transpire. If the group leader uses the affective elements expressed by the members wisely, he/she can teach the group how to couple emotions with reason. In doing so, the leader links emotional expression by group members with a cognitive understanding of the foundation for these feelings and sets the stage for profound therapeutic gains to be made within a short span of time.

A group that retains its focus on the target goals during the middle phase and a leader who values a sense of balance between the affective and cognitive factors in the group helps members coalesce and reconstitute, not fragment, during these emotionally supercharged times.

The middle or working phase allows the therapist to employ educational elements; to create experiences in the constructive expression of affect; to facilitate the acquisition of insight as well as cognitive skills; to underscore the sense of universality among members, which acts as a force that counters feelings of hopelessness and demoralization; to demonstrate the use of confrontation in a caring and sensitive way; to identify deleterious tendencies in the group, as evidenced by the members' temptation to form subgroups that have a divisive effect on the "group-as-a-whole"; and to decode the meaning of individual and group phenomena so that they can be understood more readily and employed in concert with the goals of the group.

The net effect of sensible management of the multitude of issues arising in the middle stage of managed care groups is the strengthening of group cohesion, the increased ability to focus on the work of the group on its primary tasks, and a logical and smooth progression into the termination stage of the group.

CONCURRENT REVIEW PROCESS

In managed care groups, the process of concurrent review ordinarily takes place at some point during the middle stage of the group's life. Providers may be called upon to give an update on the progress of group members towards the realization of the goals originally outlined in their initial treatment plan. A clinical example of the concurrent review process at midgroup will be presented later in this chapter as we follow the clinical course of John X., the prototypical patient used as a model throughout the text.

LEADERSHIP CONSIDERATIONS

Many of the theoretical and technical considerations that occupied the leader's focus prior to his starting the screening process for groups now play themselves out in the middle phase of the group. One method of understanding these leadership concerns can be best expressed by imagining the internal dialogue a leader has within himself/herself during points in the middle phase of a managed care group.

One common question relates to the provider's doubts about group composition: "Have I composed this group in such a way that it is operating to maximize the chances of meeting the goals for the members?" Answers to this question can be found in looking at group cohesiveness and the emotional climate in the group.

Groups that are sensibly composed should have little difficulty in establishing and maintaining a solid feeling of group cohesion. On occasion, a group member responds poorly to some aspect of the middle stage of the group and the solidarity of the group is threatened. In one short-term group for the treatment of obesity, a member balked at the leader's instruction to keep a food journal for the week. The assignment was a routine part of the group's protocol in which members are given the task of recording the time of day and exact intake of food along with some commentary about their prevailing emotional state or thoughts at the times they felt compelled to eat.

This particular member objected vigorously to the suggestion, stating that it was an invasion of privacy and an "infantilizing" request. When one member speaks in group, he/she may be echoing similar feelings held by other members. This "ventriloquist" phenomenon is common in the working stage of a homogeneous group. One person becomes the spokesperson or "mouthpiece" for the feelings of others. Members are torn in two directions between their desire for change and their corresponding fears, which propel them towards the retention of maladaptive, but familiar, dysfunctional habits or behaviors.

The leader has to be active and align with the "healthy" parts of the group membership that seek to improve their life circumstances and are willing to engage with the imagined consequences of the change process. By utilizing not only group cohesion but group pressure as well, the leader can often resolve this potential therapeutic dilemma of the oppositional behavior that is to be expected in the middle stage of the group. The leader can support the outspoken member, acknowledge the objection as an understandable one, cite the fact that fears regarding change are "normal," but also use peer pressure to get the member to abandon the oppositional stance in exchange for joining the group majority. If this happens, the member is no longer an "outsider," and it makes it much easier for the group members to lend their support during a difficult time.

The question of problems with group composition rears its head in a comparable form when a member expresses thoughts or feelings that come as a surprise to the leader and to the members. In one meeting of a managed care group for substance abuse detoxification, a member suddenly faced the leader and confronted him hostilely, accusing the leader of being an undercover police agent who was really in group to discover and turn in members who admitted to illegal drug-related behavior.

It was clear to all present that this member was much more seriously disturbed than he had appeared in the evaluation and preparation phases of the group. As a matter of fact, this particular member turned out to have a severe paranoid personality disorder, which displayed its manifestations only during the middle stage of group when the group had progressed beyond the initial stage of cohesion to a point where intermember and therapist-to-member confrontation became a regular part of the group experience. It was necessary to remove this man from group, revise his treatment plan based on the new information coming out of the group, and do a "repair" intervention with the remaining group members to help them put this experience in perspective and get back on track with the ongoing group work.

A second question a leader often asks of himself/herself during the working phase of the group is, "Have I chosen the right combination of techniques in order to bring the group along as efficiently as possible?" Managed care groups call for innovative strategies on the part of the provider. When these strategies are examined closely, they often turn out to be "therapeutic mosaics" that borrow pieces from varied schools of thought and combine them in a manner that stands the best chance of contributing to successful group outcome. The term "technical eclecticism" is one that suits the posture of the leader of a managed care group.

Sabin (1981) put this nicely in his earlier comments on the combination of factors best suited to the construction and conduct of the brief psychotherapy group: "From the encounter movement, take a good measure of optimism about the efficacy of brief group experience, so that the therapeutic power or placebo effect of the therapist's belief in the treatment will be maximized (Frank, 1973). From short-term individual psychotherapy, take a sophisticated ability to develop a sharply defined treatment focus, which will be explored intensively within the confines of brief, concentrated work (Malan, 1976; Mann, 1973; Sifneos, 1972). From long-term dynamic group psychotherapy, take skill at formulating psychological issues and treatment goals in the kind of interpersonal terms that allow both patient and therapist to understand how the group process may work (Yalom, 1975)" (pp. 280–281).

By the time the group has reached the mid-phase of its development, there should be no doubt on the provider's part regarding the choice of therapeutic ingredients involved in the treatment plan for this group. If the provider discovers that an essential piece is missing, as the group moves from being an abstract theoretical idea to an actual group in progress, the middle stage of groups still allows time to add or expand the original group design. Before the advent of concurrent review, conscientious leaders of groups were always in the habit of reviewing their work as it unfolded. Part of the advantage of not being wedded to a particular school of thought (psychoanalytic, Gestalt, Transactional Analysis, behavioral, etc.) in managed care groups is the ability it affords the provider to improvise and, like the astronaut, make "mid-flight corrections" in the group's therapeutic course.

An example of the foregoing occurred in a group of recently discharged psychiatric patients who were dealing with the issues of returning to family and work. The format was a 15-session eclectic model in which the group became stalled during sessions six and seven. Members were having difficulty in taking what they had learned in group and applying it in the outside world.

One particular member was unable to go on a job interview despite the fact that his fears about it had been voiced numerous times. The group was very sympathetic to his plight and liked him as a person. Still, this positive group climate was insufficient to mobilize the group member to actually make an appointment and go out on an actual interview. The group leader decided to use behavior rehearsal, a behavioral therapy technique involving repeated role-playing of the feared life situation in the safe, secure, and controlled setting of the group. The member did simulated interviews, with members of the group acting as the potential employer. He role-played prospective work possibilities starting with the least stressful potential situation, the accepting and welcoming interviewer, up the ladder of anxiety with the final in-group exercise involving the member playing a situation in which he was late for his appointment and had a very stern, critical, and judgmental interviewer.

When he was able to master the skills in group, only then was he encouraged to try the skills learned in group to the "real life" interview situation outside of group. He returned and reported his success in being able to overcome his fear and move forward several steps with his plans for employment. Coincidentally, since the group members played an integral part in his preparation, they enjoyed a feeling of successful participation in making a critical contribution to this member's ability to get "unstuck."

The leader's introduction of a new behavioral technique was in no way disruptive to the group, but was catalytic, not only in mobilizing the member in question but also in motivating the remaining group members to work more actively on their own goals.

The question of the choice of technical intervention that stands the best chance of working in concert with goals for the group and the individual members can also be answered when the therapist asks the question, "What level of intervention is called for at a given time?" It is virtually impossible to examine this issue without simultaneously asking oneself the corollary question, "What or who is the problem the intervention chosen is designed to remedy?"

In the managed care group, the answers to these questions lie in the provider's ability to anticipate and identify emerging problems that complicate the conduct of the group and to intervene on a level that is most specific for that particular problem. The potential levels on which interventions can be made are the individual, the interpersonal, or the whole group. The intervention chosen takes time factors into account and can be aided by a sense of on what level the emotional urgency resides in the group. One clinical vignette will help illustrate the process of choice and timing of interventions in managed care groups.

In a short-term (10-session), "communication workshop" group for married couples, an event took place which caused the leader to re-think the level of intervention most appropriate to the stage of the group. The format of this group was psychoeducational, with out-of-session "homework" for couples to practice at home and to report in subsequent group meetings only on their interaction surrounding communication. Literally one hour before the seventh group meeting, one of the husbands in the group learned that he was fired from his job. He was to meet his wife at the session and, consequently, she had no knowledge of his crisis.

His behavior in the group was withdrawn, he was uncharacteristically silent, and he appeared to be either preoccupied or depressed. As a result, several troublesome things resulted. He was unable to participate in the group assignment for that session and, perhaps more importantly, his wife assumed that the reason for his lack of participation was that he was angry with her and that she was the cause of his negative feelings. The group also felt excluded by him, and the leader was puzzled by his atypical, uncooperative group posture.

Since the behavior of an individual member was interfering with the ability of the group to make progress with its agenda, the leader decided to depart from the usual marital focus in the group to intervene on the individual level in an effort to discover the motivation for the particular group member's unusual behavior.

In response to the leader's question to the husband about his air of detachment in the group, the husband became tearful and "broke down." He really welcomed the chance to "confess" to the group that he had lost his job that evening. He went on to say that he wanted to avoid coming to the group meeting for fear that he would be seen as inadequate and as "less of a man" in everyone's eyes. The group members rallied to his support and helped him regain enough of his equilibrium to resume his participation in the group. His wife was clear about the genesis of his behavior and was also able to move towards him and reassure him that their relationship and his image in her eyes would not be damaged by his unfortunate circumstances at work.

If the leader had not shifted from the whole group level and the dyadic level of marriage, which had been the group norm, to the individual level of confronting the husband, it is probable that this would have continued to be a serious impediment to progress in the group. The individual intervention, albeit a very brief one, hit the target problem that was holding up the group.

This is one of many instances of the flexibility of group psychotherapy applied in a sensitive and timely manner and used to overcome transitory barriers to group progress. Groups always hold the potential for more than one level for therapeutic intervention and the leader who is not rigid can elect to change levels of intervention for the purpose of resolution of troublesome situations like the one just noted. Especially in managed care groups where time factors play a key role, one could easily make the case that this leadership departure from the group's customary pattern actually saved time over the course of the group's life by avoiding a situation in which the group could get bogged down for a long period of time.

Before leaving the subject of leadership concerns in the mid-phase of managed care groups, it would be worthwhile to touch upon the question that usually emerges in the leader's mind somewhere in the middle stage of both short- and long-term groups, namely, "What should be done about the uncooperative or the difficult to manage patient in the group?" Most group therapists are familiar with the inflexible roles assumed by group members. These have become so commonplace that there is a common language for the different types of "problem patients." Fixed attitudes of being help-rejecting with respect to suggestions made in the group; monopolizing members who cover their anxieties by constantly talking in group; silent members; "scapegoats"; members who attempt to gain the favor of the leader by acting like self-appointed co-therapists; self-sacrificing "martyrs", who try to gain sympathy through acts of "selflessness"; professional "victims," who are always on the losing end of experiences and relationships; and "enabling" members, who fail to see their own contributions to their current state of dissatisfaction with their lives, provide a sampling of difficult group member types.

The problem of management of these difficult patient behaviors, roles, or interpersonal styles is made more difficult in the time-limited managed care group model. Early recognition of these patterns helps the leader in two ways. First, the leader can design a clinical strategy to help the member engage directly with these problems if that is their reason for being referred for group treatment in the first place. Second, the leader who recognizes these defenses quickly stands a better chance of managing them in a way that does not permit any single member to dominate or unbalance the group through the protracted use of a countertheraputic role.

In he fifth session of a 12-session men's group, one member appeared wearing sunglasses in the session. When one of the other members asked him to remove the glasses so that they could make eye contact, he did so and revealed a large "black eye." When asked what had happened, he went into his stereotypical answer that once again he was the recipient of a mistreatment at the hands of another despite the fact that he had "done nothing wrong."

The leader chose to use this situation as a chance to concretize the fact that the member was frequently in the same position with respect to verbal interactions in the group. There was a group consensus, conveyed clearly to the member, that most of the men in the group felt he was extremely provocative in a passive way by sulking, making faces, and acting as if he were "bored" by the group. The group members agreed that he had made them angry on many occasions despite the fact that he had "done nothing wrong." The member's attachment to the group was strong and his desire for group acceptance forced him to look at his own behavior in contributing to his interpersonal conflicts.

Once he was able to entertain and acknowledge the idea that people saw him as having a less "visible" but no less critical role in creating his own troubles, the group was better able to empathize with him and help him to develop more direct ways of interacting with people. Through a process of giving advice, modeling alternative ways of handling angry feelings by "talking it out" with other group members, and learning some assertiveness skills, especially around issues involving situations in which he felt deprived or misunderstood, he was able to use the group to alter much of this heretofore troublesome behavior.

There is an imaginary spectrum along which leaders of short-term psychotherapy groups can intervene, depending upon the nature and composition of any group. As MacKenzie (1993) puts it, "The group interaction can be usefully conceptualized as lying along a continuum that at one end deals with the provision of practical support and at the other end deals with expectations of intensive introspection" (p. 426). The astute leader of managed care groups understands the capabilities of his/her group, designs goals, and plans interventions at levels attainable within the fixed time span of the group.

TRACKING PROGRESS IN MANAGED CARE GROUPS

There are two levels on which progress, or lack thereof, is measured in managed care groups: the progress of the individual group member and the progress of the group as an entity itself. To date, managed care is more concerned with tracing the clinical course of the individual in group. The process of concurrent review as currently designed is solely interested in the movement of each person in the group toward his/her original goals as set forth in the initial treatment plan.

While managed care does not require the provider to report on the group as a whole, it should not be equated with the understanding that this is an unimportant factor. Written or verbal reporting for purposes of concurrent review or mid-treatment progress reporting is for the purpose of supplying data to the managed care organization that will be helpful to them in deciding about the efficacy of treatment. The leader of the managed care group needs to think on both the individual and group level even though the reporting is done only on the former.

When the provider is alert to the issues going on in the group at the time when the concurrent review process is requested, he/she can use this information to provide invaluable data about the patient's clinical course to the managed care company. In a family issues group, for example, there will be inevitable struggles for power, competitive themes, and feelings of anger and resentment, which are inherent and "normal" parts of the group experience. If the provider is asked to report on a member's progress during the stage where the group is dealing with feelings of disappointment and deprivation at the hands of their parents, is this a normative stage of group development or is this to be reported as "patient still has problems with authority as demonstrated by expression of resentment towards parents and towards the group leader?"

Reporting individual behavior without some reference to the whole group invites misunderstanding, and even a distorted or inaccurate picture of where the patient is in his/her therapeutic course.

The above example might be better expressed as the following: "In a group that is dealing with anger directed at original family, the patient is participating actively and appropriately, although he/she is experiencing some moderate and, at times strong, feelings of depression. At this point in the group, one would expect identification and expression of these feelings rather than resolution. On that basis, he/she is making excellent progress toward the initial treatment goal of improved family relations."

With this combined individual and group model in mind, let us return to the case of John X. and see how his interim treatment report might look:

CURRENT PROBLEMS

1. Dysphoric mood (mild).
2. Substance abuse, alcohol. No current cocaine use.
3. Social isolation (diminished, has some emerging relationships).

DSM-IV Diagnosis

Axis I

Dysthymic disorder, early onset–300.4
Alcohol abuse–305.0

Axis II

No diagnosis on Axis II–V71.09

Axis III

Hypothyroidism

Axis IV

Severity of psychosocial stressors: Moderate

Axis V

Global Assessment of Functioning Score: 70

Functional Impairments

1. *Employment.* Still is unemployed but has gone on one job interview for work in an automobile repair shop.
2. *Interpersonal relationships.* Has attended all therapy appointments and has made some contacts with people attending Alcoholics Anonymous meetings. Less consumed with thoughts about his ex-girlfriend. Does not feel "ready" to contact family members.
3. *Health care.* Has seen an endocrinologist who has diagnosed him as having hypothyroidism and has started on synthetic thyroid medication.
4. *Substance abuse.* Urine testing has confirmed that he has not used cocaine since entering treatment. He still continues to use alcohol, especially in social situations. The extent of his alcohol use has diminished since his starting therapy.
5. *Mood-related issues.* Patient had difficulty with desipramine side effects of hypotension, dry mouth, and constipation. Has started on Prozac 20 mg/day and reports some lessening of depressive symptoms–sleep is better, improved ability to con-

centrate, less irritability, no suicidal ideation at present, reduction of obsessional thinking. Reports initial medication side effects of headache and diarrhea, both of which have subsided.

TARGET GOALS

1. Continue to work on remaining issues of alcohol abuse.
2. Try to broaden patient's interpersonal network in order to counter social isolation.
3. Monitor antidepressant therapy until maximum response is elicited.
4. Keep up efforts to see if family can be a resource during and after treatment.

PROPOSED INTERVENTIONS

1. Have patient continue in outpatient men's substance-abuse group for 10 more sessions. Focus will be in using the group for patient to work on interpersonal skill development and to help reduce social/interpersonal anxiety.
2. Continue daily attendance at Alcoholics Anonymous meetings. Try to obtain a sponsor in the 12-step program.
3. Continue random urine screening to assess the extent of drug use and also to reward abstinence by being able to report "clean" urine testing results in the group and in AA.
4. Recommend continuation of antidepressant medication. See if Prozac dose will need adjustment.
5. Try to arrange a family meeting to get direct observational data about family function and dysfunction. See the family "in action" to decide how they hinder or can help the recovery process.

Interim Summary

Since starting treatment, the patient has shown general progress in all areas except with his family. He is responding to antidepressant medication, attends the men's group and AA meetings on a regular basis.

He does not meet the DSM-IV criteria for Avoidant personality disorder but is shy and anxious in social situations. He is most confident when he is employed and current treatment efforts are being directed towards getting him back to work.

He has ventured out socially, mostly with people whom he has met at AA meetings.

His participation in the group has improved dramatically. He made quick identifications with other group members and is contributing on a spontaneous basis for the first time. At this stage of the group, he is attached to the experience and is a valued group member. Since the group has only recently begun to discuss their family situations, it can be anticipated that family themes will be stimulated for John X. and at that point, efforts will be made to have a meeting with all available family members.

This prototypical concurrent treatment review incorporates both group and individual elements in communicating a fuller picture to the managed care overseer. It also allows the provider to review and update the treatment plan based on its performance up to this point, assess it's efficacy, and make revisions or additions while there is still an adequate treatment timetable. The next phase of the managed care group is its journey towards termination. The tasks of this phase and the methods for managing a successful final stage of brief group treatment form the basis for the chapter to follow.

10

Termination of the Group and Follow-up Planning

GENERAL ISSUES INVOLVED IN THE TERMINATION PHASE

The issue of terminating the managed care group is an interesting phenomenon that illustrates some unique aspects of the short-term group experience. It can be argued that the level of consciousness concerning when the group will end is higher in brief group experiences than in their long-term and open-ended counterparts.

The group members' awareness of the time-limited nature of the managed care group is initiated *immediately* by the provider when he/she first mentions it during the pre-group evaluation and orientation phase.

The "psychological clock" begins ticking as soon as group leader and group member meet for the first time and both recognize the finite construction of the managed care group model. In a manner of speaking, the termination process runs concurrently with all the other stages of group development as an undercurrent known to all participants in managed care groups.

While the group is forming, becoming cohesive, setting its norms, working with specific therapeutic techniques, and resolving interpersonal issues or selected symptoms, there is a simultaneous awareness that each session brings members one step closer to the end of the group. There is no sense that time is limitless and change can take place over an undefined period as is the case in open-ended group formats. The resulting sense of urgency about time in managed care groups can be used to therapeutic advantage as a catalyst for change.

Although certain aspects of brief group therapy are unique, there are also some universal themes occurring in brief groups that are common to most forms of psychotherapy. Termination of therapy is a specific instance of this where themes of anticipated separation and loss are invariably present. Similarly, the reactivation of personal historical experiences with deaths in the members' lives or other losses of meaningful relationships almost always accompany the end of a psychotherapeutic relationship. In the termination phase of groups, losses are felt on two levels: the loss of the group therapist and the loss of the group as an entity unto itself that will never meet again.

Managed care groups are short-term experiences so that while members may become attached to one another and to the leader, it is not necessarily the same type of bonding that takes place among members of a long-term therapy group that meets over a period of years and develops a family-like atmosphere. The brevity of the work in the managed care group creates an intense but short-lived experience making for relative ease of management of the termination phase of the group.

Furthermore, the "dilution of the transference" that comes when many members share a single therapist also helps ease the pain of loss of the therapist in group as compared to individual psychotherapies. Since successful group experiences teach group members how to rely on peers as well as on authority figures, members who are leaving the managed care group do so with enhanced interpersonal skills. This provides the basis for finding and forming rewarding relationships with peers in their personal and professional lives once the group is over.

Termination in managed care groups is unique in the fact that all group participants terminate at the same time. This process of universal termination for all members singles out no particular group member and in so doing helps avoid undue feelings of competition and failure as seen in long-term groups when one member reaches his/her goals and departs while others remain on in the group.

A further caveat to the provider during the termination stage of managed care groups is to stick to the original time frame no matter what pressure the group exerts to extend the sessions. While this may be patently obvious, the group leader is far from immune to the forces at play in groups and may be tempted to depart from the agreed upon therapeutic plan.

There appear to be at least two ways of understanding how the termination phase can become a problematic one for the provider of managed care group services. The articulation and sense of identification between aspects of the therapist's personality and a particular group or group member often forms the basis for the leader's temptation to extend the group time module. This psychodynamically derived "countertransferential blind spot" is perhaps better known than its social systems counterpart, the concept of the therapist becoming influenced by the power of the system and succumbing to group pressure by departing from his/her designated leadership role and goals.

In either case, the leader is wise to consider and discuss the time issue openly for the therapeutic value it has in helping members to better understand the emotional impact of termination in the group. Leaders should take pains to conduct the group in a way such that they will not find themselves in the unenviable position of making policy changes late in the life of the group. If this unfortunately happens, not only does the therapist's credibility suffer but the group itself is not given a vote of confidence for its positive accomplishments that have been designed specifically to help them cope with life's transitions, separations, and losses.

Brief groups conducted under the auspices of managed care also provide members with an opportunity to review their target goals and to see how close they have come to reaching them. While the review is ideally cast in positive terms, it should never be at the expense of the truth. Managed care groups may be excellent avenues for effective short-term treatment, but they are not a panacea. At termination, all members review their group experience and some are likely to be further along than others. Group members who need further therapy have their cases reviewed by the leader who then confers with the managed care reviewer in discussing further treatment options, family, community, and other resources that may be needed as an extension of the work done in the short-term group.

In the managed care substance-abuse group, which has been used as an example of a key part of the treatment plan for John X., the issues surrounding termination would include: total abstinence from all mind- and mood-altering substances, the attainment of a clear sense of individual and group identity, a facility with effective interpersonal communication, a knowledge of self-monitoring skills to identify potential risk factors for repeated substance abuse, an acknowledgement of emotional issues linked to separation, and a concrete plan for remaining abstinent from drugs and alcohol after exiting from the group.

Follow-up planning and the scheduling of contacts with the leader at specified intervals after the group ends is the other critical part of the termination phase. Although actual follow-up takes place after the group has concluded, the planning for aftercare or follow-up visits is done during the termination stage of the group.

Individual meetings with former group members held after the group has finished are for purposes of insuring that positive change is being maintained in order to reinforce it and to assess the need for any further treatment, and for purposes of data collection referable to outcome studies of treatment efficacy.

EVOLUTION OF CURRENT PRACTICES INVOLVING GROUP TERMINATION

Historically, it was common to see group therapy programs in outpatient settings have a large roster of groups that were never reviewed with an eye towards termination. Many of these groups were in existence for years and had many of the charter members still present. Still other groups had a shifting membership over time, but the original purpose and direction of the group had been lost. In institutions where there is a staff turnover, as in facilities with training programs as part of their mission, changes of therapist occur regularly, often with inadequate communication between incoming and departing leaders. Therapists who "inherited" an established group had little or no sense of the group's history and were frequently confused as to the genesis of problems being encountered by the new leader in the group.

Although there is a bona fide case that can be made for keeping chronically ill psychiatric patients in long-term, open-ended therapy groups, this is best done by design, not by default. A treatment plan for a chronic schizophrenic patient who has a history of multiple psychiatric hospitalizations can be one in which the patient is placed in a "maintenance group therapy" program. The goals in this model are to avoid repeated hospitalization, to keep the patient from being socially isolated, to monitor the patient's need for medication, and to see the patient interact in the interpersonal sphere of the group so that early intervention can take place before the patient reaches a state of deterioration necessitating an inpatient stay.

One of the most important lessons to come out of the study of neverending, unexamined outpatient groups is that there is no reason to believe that longer means better unless the groups are periodically reassessed. This entails a regular review of the group membership, attendance, goals, current focus of the group, and an estimate of when the group will be terminating. In so doing, many facilities have done a sorely needed "editing" function in their group therapy programs. This has not only upgraded the quality of patient care but has also led to greater diversity of group service delivery.

Focused, brief therapy groups have been born out of this process in many centers. Fragmented groups of insufficient size have been closed; groups that were limping along with a demoralized membership and leadership have come up for review and have either been re-vitalized with new members and a clearly defined sense of purpose or a decision has been made to terminate the group and make alternative treatment dispositions for the members. Moreover, a host of short-term, theme-oriented groups has been added to these programs. Staff and patient enthusiasm invariably improves as the prospect of group treatment becomes less vague and amorphous. The expansion of the time-efficient group modality has led to a corresponding sense of greater awareness of issues arising in the termination phase of brief groups.

An outline of termination phase considerations for the provider (see Table 3) will form the remainder of this chapter.

Dies (1994) cautions that the therapist leading the group through the termination phase should be on the alert "not to allow members to bog down in excessive emotionality or to remain withdrawn and closed off from their affective experiences. Nor is this a time to attempt extensive individual therapeutic work or to open new issues" (p. 94). The focal point for the provider who is trying to help the group end therapeutically has to be on identifying and processing the strong feelings that emerge during this phase.

One part of this task is for the leader to differentiate between those feelings stimulated by the group termination and those indicative of other unresolved issues. Other problems emerging during the termination phase, but not in direct response to it, must be labelled as indi-

TABLE 3

Termination Stage

	Long-term group	*Managed Care Group*
Length of time	Many sessions; "ritualization" and long preparation phase	Shorter, more sudden termination
Awareness of group ending	Late in the life of the group	Immediate and ongoing
Group cohesion	Stronger, longer duration of cohesion	Shorter, intense sense of cohesion
Common themes	Separation, death, loss	Separation, death, unfinished business
Periodic review of therapy	Sometimes	Always
Timing of termination	Members end singly when individual goals have been met	Whole group ends at the same time
Transference	"Family-like"; central to the technique in psychodynamic groups	Present but not as developed as in psychodynamic groups. Not always regarded as useful method
Group focus	May shift over time	Persistent focus on original group goal
Therapist "risks"	Countertransference problems	Extending the ending date of the group
Follow-up	Usually, unless group alone is sufficient therapy plan	Always done as part of the group itself

vidual material that has yet to be resolved and/or is beyond the scope of the brief therapy group. The follow-up plan for members in this category is the place in which residual psychological problems are addressed and a plan for their management in further therapy is made when necessary.

Members who miss the last session provide a clinical example of the kind of extreme behavior that signals the provider that more work needs to be done. Some members have such profound difficulties with saying "good-bye," finalizing, and not denying the ending of life experiences that they feel compelled to absent themselves from the parallel experience of the parting of the group in the last session.

Another issue stimulated by the ending of the group is the request by members to have a celebration or party to mark the end of the group. This occurs in both short- and long-term groups and is a piece of clinical behavior that is worthy of serious analysis by the group leader. It is the author's experience that a termination "party" in either type of group is best handled by using it to underscore the work of the group and as direct behavioral data emanating from patients and telegraphing their feelings about the end of the group rather than to see it on a more superficial level and simply grant or deny the request without having made an effort to grasp its significance.

The termination phase is a phase during which strong ambivalent feelings about many issues are felt and often enacted. The effective group leader needs to understand the late-stage group behavior of each individual and of the group as a whole. Members have mixed feelings about having no choice in the decision regarding whether or not the group continues. They also have conflicted emotions towards the leader as well as to their peers in the group. They are frequently fearful about the prospect of living life without the support of the group to fall back on.

Some of the negative feelings in relationship to the leader are traceable to a sense of "incompleteness" and resentment directed at the therapist, who is seen as having been inadequate to help a member resolve enough problems during the course of the group. Both direct and indirect expressions of ambivalence are present throughout the course of the brief therapy group, as well as in the final session. Having a party or celebration at a time when many members are feeling emotionally conflicted about the cessation of group meetings helps obscure rather than clarify many important issues for members.

From a purely time-efficient standpoint, managed care and brief therapy groups are so short in duration that leaders can use all the time they can get to do the therapeutic work of the group. Being parsimonious about time factors is not equivalent to being insensitive to the requests, realistic or unrealistic, made by members. It merely means that if the issues remaining to be dealt with for the membership can best be resolved by full use of the last meeting, then that remains the priority for the group and leader.

Despite the fact that the leader may clearly explain the rationale for opting not to have a closing party, it is usually safe to assume that many members will still have feelings of disappointment, anger, and frustration alongside their intellectual understanding of the leader's reasons for the decision. Piper (1992), in his short-term group work with depression and loss, used the term "judgment day" to express the perception by members about the final session of the group. When viewed in this context, the last meeting of the group can be a point of celebration for some while for others it may be more akin to a funeral. Piper's observations add weight to the decision to formalize the ending of the group by some means other than having a farewell party.

Alternative ways of concretizing the ending of groups without interfering with the psychological and psychodynamic factors at play in the termination stage have been proposed by several authors who suggest a closing exercise or ritual as a way of delineating the end of the group. Practically speaking, the last session can be one in which the leader encourages the appropriate physical gestures surrounding parting from a significant relationship. This usually takes the form of "handshakes and hugs" in many instances.

Choosing a closing exercise at the beginning of a last group session mobilizes, rather than inhibits, the expression of feelings present around termination. The advantage of starting a final group in this way is that it forces the emotions felt by members out into the open atmosphere of the group and still allows time during the rest of the session to deal directly with anticipated issues of grief, fears about self-sufficiency, loss, and other important emotional themes.

Rutan and Stone (1993) wisely note that in groups "the leavetaking is more public." For many departing group members, this adds the extra dimension of potential feelings of failure in comparison to others in the group and interpersonal anxieties centering about feelings of embarrassment for openly displaying feelings of sadness, or crying, or fear of being viewed by the members and the leader as unable to be emotionally mature enough to cope with the termination of a group experience. This rich field of significant emotional reactions to separation and loss provides the member and therapist with a rare opportunity for both experiential and cognitive learning to transpire in the final group meeting.

The termination phase, and a portion of the last session in particular, can be used as an avenue for work on intermember themes. In managed care groups, the last session includes a review of progress towards the group and individual goals. As noted earlier, this process is cast in a realistic but favorable light. It is an appropriate time for members to express their gratitude to others in the group who have been helpful to them. Additionally, the last session gives the group provider a chance to emphasize the cooperative spirit in the group and how each member's participation was an integral part of the successful goals reached over the course of the group. This helps reward mutual cooperation and enhances the self-esteem of group members.

When members are on the brink of venturing back out into the "real world," the increased sense of self-worth and the acquisition of improved cooperative skills help offset many fears members have about going away from the group without the interpersonal "tools" necessary for survival and for fruitful involvements with others in relationships.

The maxim of work done in the group having to be applied to life outside of group has been central to brief group therapy. One can see the benefits of this group norm when it comes time to end the group. Members have already begun to do the work required in "life after group" during each session and in the time between meetings of the group. This is invaluable in offsetting the fear that group is an artificial world and helps members engage more readily in outside activities.

Some managed care groups work in a structured format and have a specific protocol for each session of the group. Rice (1995) has conducted structured, 12-session groups for the treatment of depression. The management of termination in this group model follows a predetermined course of goals and guidelines that encompasses a method for dealing with many of the familiar issues associated with the ending of the group.

A typical twelfth or final session has three goals: "(1) To evaluate the personal and group aspects of the therapy experience. (2) To review goal attainment. (3) To create a positive termination atmosphere" (pp. 95–96). In order to realize these goals, Rice divides the last session into two parts, consisting of group discussion and group activities. The questions for group discussion are: "What changes do you see in yourself since the group began? What have you learned and accomplished? How can you maintain your gains? What are your feelings about the group ending?" (p. 96).

The group activity portion of the final session is one during which members "share positive changes." The action components that accompany this segment include: "Each member sharing his or her positive changes and taping them to a poster or wall. The leader participates in this activity by talking about the changes he or she sees in each member. Individual goals are reviewed." As an alternative group activity, members can write down their impressions about other group members on a piece of paper and give the paper to the member who is the subject of the comments.

One can look at termination and its management through many windows of the therapeutic "greenhouse." Consensus exists, independent of which window, or professional point of view, one looks through, that terminating the managed care group requires thoughtfulness, planning, and sensitivity on the part of the provider. When these factors are sensibly combined into a treatment plan, the chances for creating a productive ending to the group are increased considerably.

Details about follow-up planning and implementation will be dealt with in greater depth in Chapter 13 in the discussion of themes related to therapeutic outcome in brief psychotherapy groups.

Part III

Special Issues

11

The Inpatient Group and Groups with Unique Patient Populations

Up to this point, the outpatient group has been the prototype group for the managed care model. However, outpatient groups of short duration are indicated for only a portion of the mentally ill population. In this section, three different aspects of group treatment under managed care will be discussed in order to offer some thoughts about how best to incorporate the treatment of other patients into the managed care model.

Just as traditional models of long-term group psychotherapy had to be modified to meet the demands of contemporary mental health care, so too will aspects of the managed care group models described thus far have to be modified, liberalized, and adjusted if they are to meet the needs of a broad range of patients in need of quality care.

In order to provide a cross-sectional view of the challenges facing managed care groups and some possible solutions to the problems they will encounter, three parameters have been chosen for purposes of illustration: *a setting*: the inpatient ward of the hospital; *a patient population*: patients with personality disorders; and *a technique*: the use of structured protocols in the treatment of a variety of psychological conditions. In this format, it will be possible to address some of the "special cases" for which the conventional brief therapy group will not suffice.

MANAGED CARE GROUPS IN THE HOSPITAL SETTING

The Inpatient Psychiatric Service

A group experience of some kind is a regular component of the overall treatment plan for almost every psychiatric patient whose condition is serious enough to warrant hospitalization. Whether it is a large group like a community meeting on a milieu therapy service, an occupational therapy group, an art or music therapy program, or a psychotherapy group per se, each psychiatric inpatient usually comes in contact with a form of interpersonal therapeutic endeavor as part of the hospital stay.

Lengthy inpatient psychiatric hospitalization is the most costly form of psychological care. As such, managed care companies, HMOs, insurance companies, and others concerned with cost-containment of mental health care service delivery are increasingly interested in cutting costs in this area. Inpatient groups can play a key role towards this end if they are designed and carried out in a creative way.

There is a substantial literature on group therapy with psychiatric inpatients that is far too broad to summarize here and still do justice to the subject. For the reader interested in more depth about this subject, Kibel (1993a) has reviewed this literature in an overview well worth reading for anyone involved with the inpatient group.

There is, on the other hand, a veritable absence of articles addressing issues at the interface between inpatient group experiences and managed mental health care. In order to shed some light on this subject, it will be helpful to review three prominent inpatient group orientations, examine some of their essential aspects, and discuss how to employ some of their central elements in an attempt to bring them in line with current managed care standards.

Although there is a significant dispute concerning the question of whether or not psychodynamically oriented groups can be effective with very disturbed patients on a short-stay inpatient service, there are exponents of this view who have written quite convincingly about the subject. Rice and Rutan (1987) have tried to conceptualize the inpatient group along psychodynamic lines due to their concern that, "the psychodynamic understanding of psychological illness is losing ground in favor of newer, presumably quicker and more cost-efficient treatments. In the process, we feel patients are often misunderstood and mistreated, and the richness and complexity of human experience are minimized" (p. vii).

Their model encompasses a technique that has at its core a belief that the basic goal of the inpatient group is to, "enable the members to begin reestablishing clear interpersonal boundaries and connections" (p. 91). The system they have created in order to effectuate this goal is a series of group experiences based on the current level of function of a given inpatient. The patients functioning at the lowest levels are placed in a Level I group, which strives to provide an atmosphere of acceptance for patients, help them regain a sense of emotional equilibrium, and assist them in making minimal efforts at making interpersonal connections with others in the group.

The Level II group is for the patient who shows no signs of active suicidal intent, dangerousness, or psychosis and is reintegrating psychologically. The goals of these groups are to keep the patients moving in a stable and progressive direction, to teach them how to relate constructively to others, and to begin to introduce the notion of the connection between current behaviors or current problems with their current life circumstances outside of the hospital.

As one might expect, the Level III group includes members who are far along enough in their recovery to be considered as candidates for discharge from the hospital. Planning and facilitating the transition to outpatient care, return to family, and work-related issues form some focal themes of the Level III group.

In all groups of this kind, patients agree to abide by a basic therapeutic contract, which includes agreement to attend and stay through all group meetings; to be punctual in arriving at sessions; to keep the confidence of group members by agreeing not to discuss group-related issues with other patients on the ward who are not in the group; to be open about discussing extra-group contacts with other members between sessions; and to communicate in safe and appropriate ways, namely by talking, not enacting, their thoughts and feelings.

The psychodynamic aspects of this technique combine the use of transference relationships in the group and employing metaphors as a device for helping patients understand their emotions, conflicts, interpersonal patterns, and intrapsychic issues. The leader provides not only a facilitative role but a role of clarifier in an effort to help severely disturbed patients attribute accurate meaning and interpretation to group events.

The work just noted is done with the higher functioning hospitalized patients and was originally done in a setting where time was not restricted. This may account for some of the success in using modified psychodynamic group principles with a patient population not usually expected to benefit from more traditional approaches.

Rice and Rutan have done more than merely transpose psychoanalytically derived group theory and practice to the inpatient group. They value the social systems view of the hospital as a large group, demonstrate a sensitivity to recognizing the adaptive capacities and limitations of each group member, and underscore critical issues of treating the seriously ill inpatient with respect and dignity. These elements have been intelligently combined to result in an updated psychodynamic therapeutic approach to inpatient group psychotherapy that has much to offer the managed care provider who leads a group of higher functioning psychiatric inpatients.

The second prototypical model for inpatient group psychotherapy comes from Yalom's (1983) interpersonal and experiential system. Broadly speaking, Yalom views time as the essence of every group meeting on the short-term inpatient service. Since length of stay is getting shorter and patient turnover is occurring at an increasingly rapid rate, Yalom's thinking about groups in short-length-of-stay settings has special significance to the system of managed care. The two models parallel each other closely with respect to brevity and economy of treatment and with limited exposure time for the therapist to work with the patient.

One of the highlights of this therapeutic orientation is the view that each session is a self-contained entity with its own stages, goals, group dynamics, and leadership tasks. The group leader has to imagine that there is only one session in which to work, and that every group session is a "therapy in miniature." Due to the rapidly shifting membership and the degree of disturbance of the participants, it is difficult, if not impossible, to establish a sense of continuity of group themes or relationships from session to session on the short-term acute psychiatric service.

Prompted by these and other observations about the limitations surrounding inpatient groups, Yalom devised a system that has patients establishing goals for themselves in every session of the inpatient group. This is followed by a plan for the implementation of that goal in the same session. Depending upon the level of functioning of any patient, the goal can be as simple as learning the names of two other group members, making eye contact with the leader or fellow group members, or remaining seated throughout the full group session.

Principles that are highly valued by managed care, including goal specificity, effective use of time, and psychotherapeutic interventions that are definable, measurable, and teachable, are all essential parts of Yalom's approach to inpatient group work. Equally if not more important is the sense of immediate accomplishment and heightened group morale. By working in a concrete way that models a beginning, middle, and end of life experiences, and an ability to understand important aspects of human relationships, the inpatient group can impart tangible benefits directly to members of these groups.

The orientation of these groups is in the present and discourages forays into the patient's past life in the manner that traditional long-term psychodynamic groups espouse. Other features emblematic of this method include a recommendation for daily or very frequent group meetings, active leadership around establishing and mainaintaining the group focus, and an effort to keep the group centered on an interactional plane using the in-group transactions in the here-and-now as the major medium through which the therapeutic process is mediated.

Yalom's use of the phrase, "a consistent, coherent group procedure" with an emphasis on elements of safety, security, and control dovetails nicely with the governing precepts of the managed care model.

A third way of studying the inpatient group is from the general systems theory vantage point. This view considers the hospital as a large social system, the inpatient ward as a smaller subsystem of that larger unit, and the inpatient therapy group as yet another microcosm of the system. Conceptualizing the group experience as one dimension of the larger system is a valuable way of understanding issues and problems arising at any level of the system as manifested on the "local" level of the inpatient group. When one understands the dynamics of the small group, it can be seen as means of taking a "psychological biopsy" of the total system.

Problems with the hospital in general, such as how the psychiatric service is regarded by those in positions of power and decision making; issues on the particular ward, such as a low regard for group as compared to other psychotherapies or to medication; individual issues, including patient reluctance to join or participate in group; and internal staff conflicts can all be seen reflected in the transactions of the inpatient therapy group

Some of the specific elements concerning the construction, conduct, and problems associated with this systems model have been astutely described by Kibel (1993a,b) and are very helpful in conceptualizing the clinical and practical considerations in the work ahead for a provider who leads managed care groups. He speaks specifically to the issue of goal setting of the inpatient group. On the general level, Kibel (1993b) sees the leader's goals as using, "support and structure, active facilitation by the therapist, problem spotting and problem solving.... All these methods aim to rapidly reduce the problematic behavior that led to hospitalization" (p. 90).

Five specific goals comprise the essence of his view of the value of inpatient group experiences. Goals are seen on a continuum ranging from basic or survival needs to higher levels of patient function primarily concerned with "quality of life" issues. As he states them, the goals are in ascending order: "(1) Engaging patients in conversation and promoting conversation among them. (2) Making the group interactive so that it can serve as an instrument for peer support and assistance. (3) Using the group to cultivate an atmosphere of open communication on the unit. (4) Bringing for discussion and clarifying milieu issues so as to make the social system of the unit comprehensible to the patients. (5) Relieving and correcting negative transference reactions to the group leader, which function as a paradigm for all patient-staff relationships" (Kibel, 1993a, pp. 102–103).

The three systems approach the inpatient therapy group from slightly different positions. However, it is evident that all have a healthy respect for the delicate balance between stability and disorganization in patients; all attempt to meet the patients at their level and gradually move them in the direction of greater psychological understanding and personal integration; all pay attention to the here-and-now level of the group; all view the inpatient group as part of a larger social system that has to be understood in terms of its facilitative or obstructionistic function in relationship to the small inpatient group; and all acknowledge that group is an essential part, but only a part, of a comprehensive treatment plan for the psychiatric inpatient.

No discussion of inpatient groups would be complete without enumerating several other themes influencing the in composition of the group. The role of medication management has to be given careful thought. Many inpatient groups are "medication groups" wherein the prescribing and the monitoring of side effects and beneficial effects form the content of the group sessions. When someone other than the group leader is overseeing the patient's psychopharmacological portion of the treatment plan, an arrangement for open communication between group leader and medication manager is essential. There are also very significant feelings and psychodynamic issues related to medication in groups that one should not overlook by merely leading a group that only checks symptoms (Rodenhauser, 1989; Zaslav & Kalb, 1989).

One of the cardinal goals of all managed care groups is to try to get patients to "like the group experience." What this means when it is successful is that a patient who has either had a positive inpatient group experience or, at minimum, has learned through group participation not to be afraid of groups is much more likely to continue outpatient care that includes a group therapy component. Such patients are less likely to get lost in the transition from inpatient to outpatient treatment and thereby lower the overall dropout rate for follow-up treatment in general. Getting patients to experience and enjoy group therapy is a clear, modest, and invaluable aspiration for the provider. It also counters leadership demoralization born out of the mistake of setting goals that are too ambitious for the inpatient population, thus invariably disappointing the therapist and creating a hazard for severely disturbed patients.

Finally, a word should be said about the broad applicability of hospital groups in accommodating patients in a wide range of diagnostic conditions. Schizophrenic patients may be the most commonly hospitalized group of patients, but they are by no means the only cluster of patients for whom the brief inpatient group is useful. Groups of patients with bipolar affective disorders (Kanas, 1993) serve as a model for conducting treatment groups with seriously impaired patients in homogeneous groupings. These groups can be set in either the inpatient or outpatient venues depending on the degree of severity of the current condition of each group member. Their aim is to help patients understand their shared psychological symptoms and to elicit greater treatment compliance among the membership.

In sum, the inpatient setting, once thought to be a place for only "warehousing" very disturbed psychiatric patients, has become a critical and exciting place to begin the treatment process for many patients. The managed care group based on the model of the short-term, rapid turnover system has much to offer in this process.

THE HOSPITALIZED PATIENT WITH A MEDICAL ILLNESS

The practice of group psychotherapy has changed dramatically over the past few decades. Contemporary group approaches reflect the tremendous growth, expansion, and research efforts that have taken place in the field. One impressive area where the results of this work can be seen is in the application of time-limited group experiences for patients who are medically ill enough to require hospitalization.

For purposes of clarity, group work with medical patients can be viewed as having at least two major goals: to help members cooperate with medical and surgical treatment plans and to define and treat psychological factors that either contribute etiologically to, or are by-products of, serious medical illness. Stress reduction and the acquisition of relaxation or stress management skills form the mainstay of these groups.

The array of conditions and types of patients for which groups have been designed is far-reaching. A partial list of group work currently in progress includes groups for patients with coronary artery disease, AIDS, multiple sclerosis, irritable bowel syndrome, Type A behavior, asthma, psoriasis, cancer, hypertension, kidney transplants, arthritis, and chronic pain syndromes. Groups have also been formed for post-operative amputees, children with cerebral palsy or other neurological conditions, and patients on kidney dialysis (Spitz, 1984). For a more detailed description of this model, the work of Kelly et al. (1993) with support groups for depressed HIV patients and of Forester et al. (1993) with group therapy for patients receiving radiotherapy are excellent examples for further reading about the rationale and conduct of groups for somatic illness.

Groups for medically ill patients share many common features. The overwhelming majority are homogeneous in composition for an illness shared by all members. This homogeneity of group composition facilitates destigmatization and earlier entry into psychological treatment.

Common group themes can be used to engage patients who frequently resent defining themselves as being in need of psychological help and who are at high risk to drop out of conventional individual psychotherapy. Consequently, one of the central goals of all these groups is to offer a more palatable way for medically ill patients to avail themselves of sorely needed treatment for their emotional ills.

Short-term groups for medically ill patients strive to help patients live more realistically and comfortably with their conditions. The peer support and staff support elements of the group are important influences toward this end. Group membership helps counter negative feelings of uniqueness, freakishness, disfigurement, and social isolation while simultaneously preserving and bolstering the patient's self-esteem. A health care staff that is sensitive to the emotional vulnerabilities of the medically ill patient is essential to the accomplishment of this goal.

One focal point of group discussion often is the impact of a chronic or debilitating disease on individuals and families. Most group leaders make an organized effort to constructively involve families and support systems in the therapeutic process. Encouragement of clear and open communication among patients, families, and the health care team is an intrinsic element of these group approaches.

Certain general principles extracted from studies on groups conducted in the hospital setting with patients diagnosed as having serious cardiovascular disease provide a set of guidelines that most therapists accept as helpful in treating the medically ill patient. These findings are: that early intervention is highly valued; that spouses, family, and significant others should be involved in the treatment plan; that group leaders need not necessarily be physicians, but should be professionals who are informed about physical and psychological risk factors; and that many physically ill patients are ill-suited to intensive, insight-oriented, long-term individual psychotherapies and are better managed in groups emphasizing supportive, educative, and behavioral components.

Groups are particularly helpful in monitoring the psychological state of the medically ill patient. Therapeutic groups are an unsurpassed milieu for observing interactional as well as individual behavior. Group support tends to offset feelings of despair and dysphoria while at the same time providing a constructive counseling setting for the dissemination to patients of the most current information about their conditions. Groups are also noteworthy for their ability to be a resource for helping patients make life-style modifications that will augment the quality of life for the patient.

Many programs advocate the use of adjunctive, focal groups as part of the overall management of the medically ill patient. These groups are time-limited and follow a cognitive/behavioral model targeted at specific symptoms or habits. For the coronary-prone patient, such groups address smoking cessation, weight control, alcohol use, and relaxation or meditation training. Often, these groups deal with specific concerns of the post-coronary patient and discuss issues such as resuming an active sexual life, devising a sensible diet and exercise program, and planning for a gradual return to work.

The essential spirit of these groups for patients with serious and/or chronic medical conditions is contained in Spiegel and Yalom's (1978) work with groups of women in the terminal stages of breast cancer. They described the purpose of the group for the hospitalized medically ill patient as being one of helping members, "to plan and live through the remainder of their lives with an enhanced sense of meaning and dignity" (p. 244).

GROUPS FOR PATIENTS WITH PERSONALITY DISORDERS

How will proponents of managed mental health care engage with the problems posed by patients with a DSM-IV diagnosis of personality disorder? Whether or not these patients can be effectively treated in any form of brief therapy is a controversial question in itself. Moreover, since most psychotherapeutic treatment of patients with personality disorders has been very long-term, psychodynamically oriented, individual psychotherapy, what role is there for group therapy in adding something to the notoriously difficult task of treating these patients psychotherapeutically? Beyond that, even where groups can be helpful in some ways, must they also be long-term, costly models?

These are but a few of the questions facing the provider in a managed care system with a significant percentage of its patient pool composed of patients in this diagnostic category. The focus here will be on delineating the contribution that can be made by therapeutic groups for patients with personality disorders and on raising some questions for future study in this area.

The person with a borderline personality disorder may be one of the most challenging patients to treat and will serve as the example to be used here, in part because there is the largest literature on this condition as opposed to other Axis II diagnoses. Several authors have addressed core aspects of treating borderline patients in the group setting or in combined individual and group psychotherapy.

Kibel (1980) and Roth (1982) both stress the views of many experienced group therapists who advocate intensive pre-group screening of borderline patients in order to prevent their inappropriate placement in groups. Intrapsychic, interpersonal, and environmental factors, ego strengths, temperament, character traits, psychological mindedness, and motivation for treatment comprise a "short list" of factors to be evaluated prior to group placement. Roth also offers a typology for characterizing borderline and narcissistic patients who are functioning at a lower level as an aid in determining whether or not a patient is suitable for group therapy.

Wong (1980a,b), Stone and Gustafson (1982), Macaskill (1982), and Horwitz (1977) address theoretical and pragmatic aspects of the actual group process for the borderline patient. Wong conceptualizes the group work as having five focal issues: defining the diagnostic criteria clearly, choosing between supportive and reconstructive treatment, deciding whether or not to combine individual and group psychotherapy, choosing to have homogeneous (all members are borderline personality disorders) versus heterogeneous group composition (groups of mixed diagnostic states), and considering the possibility of more than one group experience over time.

Stone and Gustafson, as well as Roth, offer conceptual frameworks for better understanding the interventions used in these groups. They concentrate on issues of technique, such as facilitating entry for the borderline patient, using noninterpretive therapist activity, differentiating between group phenomena of cohesion and idealization, and constructively using confrontation and empathy. Roth uses object-relations theory to illustrate how the leader's countertransference responses can be used to tap the rich field of interpersonal distortions so common among borderline patients in group therapy.

Macaskill attempted to illuminate the issue of which technical interventions are most and least useful to borderline patients in a one-year outpatient psychotherapy group. His work and the work of others more recently, such as Segal and Weideman (1995) and Marziali and

Munroe-Blum (1994), have addressed the issues of leadership role, application of interpersonal group psychotherapeutic techniques to borderline patient groups, and management of leader and member relationships within the therapy groups.

The consensus of many of these studies is strikingly similar to Horwitz's (1977) original rationale for the use of groups for the borderline patient in which he expressed the following reasons for considering group treatment: Groups provide multiple "targets," or part-objects, as personified by the other group members, enabling the external world of the group to more closely mirror the internal world of object relations experienced by borderline patients; groups allow the borderline member more room to hide when needed due to the presence of other members with whom the leader is shared; group therapy is an excellent setting for reality testing, boundary definition, limit setting, and delay of individual gratification; groups help guide members toward more socially appropriate interpersonal responses through the feedback and modeling that take place regularly; the added possibilities for positive identifications not only with the therapist but with peers helps reinforce a sense of adult identity in the group membership; and group can be stimulating and involving for the more withdrawn or fearful person with a borderline personality disorder.

To this author's knowledge, there is no scientific basis for believing that thorough treatment of patients with personality disorders can be accomplished in a brief group therapy model. This is not meant to imply that groups do not have a significant role in treatment, but rather that groups are used to greatest advantage when they are specific for a set of behaviors or symptoms commonly found among patients with serious personality disorders.

One way of conceptualizing the role of groups for patients with personality disorders is to take a longitudinal view of the patient's need for treatment over his/her life span and to ask the question: What group would be best, at what time in the patient's development or clinical course, to address what specific attitudes, behaviors, or symptoms? Thinking along these lines accomplishes several things for the patient and the therapist.

The therapist is immediately relieved of the burden of total responsibility for "fixing" the borderline patient. I prefer a view in which the psychotherapeutic work necessary for borderline patients is "subcontracted" out to more than one provider. In this model, the provider of group services can effectively use some of the brief group therapy experiences to deal with only a portion of the overall care the borderline patient will require in his/her treatment lifetime.

If the group focus is narrowed, there is usually a corresponding lowering of the anxiety level of the patient, which stems from a sense of ambiguity, lack of structure, close proximity to the therapist, fears of one's own or other group members' impulses getting out of control, and similar concerns that are all addressed routinely in the contemporary brief group therapy model.

Two of the studies cited above help illustrate the application of the principle of "subcontracting" in group therapy for borderline patients. In Segal and Weideman's (1995) group format, the emphasis is on interpersonal positions adopted by borderline patients. In their words, "The organizing perspective we take is that the patients relate through a specific interactional pattern that involves the patient's adopting one of two major stances–competence versus incompetence" (p. 157). The aim of this group model is more behavioral than characterological as it tries to resolve "an unstable split between conflicting poles of the self system" (p. 157).

In practical terms, these groups consist of a core of nuclear group members and a rotating group of "satellite" members who attend the group less regularly. The average length of treatment is less than one year and the drop-out rate is high. Leaders in these groups make a decided effort to remain 'consistent, interested, empathic yet neutral." This therapist posture is felt to be a stabilizing, nonintrusive influence on the group and functions to reduce excessive affect and provide a "holding environment" for the membership. Interpretive interventions are avoided owing to a concern about their greater potential to stimulate and potentially destabilize the balance between self-states of competence and incompetence.

Marziali and Munroe-Blum (1994) employ a 25-session (and five later sessions spaced at two-week intervals) format that applies the interpersonal psychotherapeutic approach in a time-limited format for patients with a diagnosis of borderline personality disorder. One of the most interesting aspects of their technique is the rationale they supply for putting a time limit on the group treatment of the borderline patient. They value the ability of time-limited groups to "protect against severe therapeutic regressions that are more apt to occur when the borderline patient becomes exclusively dependent for survival on one therapist and the therapy" (p. 68). Furthermore, they state that, "A time boundary, set prior to treatment, provides a secure and reassuring structure, especially for borderline patients whose expectations about the constancy of persons of trust have been frequently frustrated" (p. 68).

The technique used in the group relies heavily on the replication of old interpersonal patterns in the new context of the group where it is easier to identify them and to search for more adaptive alternative behaviors. The stance of the therapist in this model is described as one of "noninterpretive, empathic feedback" and the approach differs from others frequently used with borderline members in avoiding direct or harsh confrontation in the group.

Both these examples raise some unsolved questions for the treatment of patients with Axis II diagnoses under managed care guidelines. The terms "brief" and "time-limited" take on new meaning and are obviously much "longer" than the 10-session or 12-session brief group therapy paradigm so popular today. Practitioners of these group methods claim they are cost-effective because they provide a clear and circumscribed agenda addressing only one or two aspects of dysfunction in the current life of the borderline patient.

In these models it is perfectly acceptable and expected that patients with personality disorders will require several treatment interventions over time. It is argued that the more specific the goals, the less confusing the group will be for both provider and patient. It is not only fine from a psychological standpoint, but from a cost-efficiency point of view as well, according to this philosophy of treatment, for a patient to be in sequential, concentrated forms of brief therapy from time to time in preference to years of ongoing individual psychotherapy.

With respect to managed care, the case may be as simple as acknowledging that "special patients" require "special treatments." The concept of what constitutes an *effective* therapeutic experience for a person with a personality disorder is more relevant than the time it takes to complete that treatment and whether or not therapy is conducted "in one sitting" or intermittently over a period of years. In either case, brief managed care groups offer enormous options to the provider who works with a patient with the chronic and often unstable features of an Axis II diagnosis.

STRUCTURED MANAGED CARE GROUP MODELS

Prior to our leaving the subject of variations on the theme of the managed care group model, it would be prudent to include a synopsis of some of the work being done in groups with fixed time spans that have a specific treatment protocol for each group session. These structured group experiences are demonstrating an applicability to a range of psychological conditions and to an even broader array of maladaptive behaviors and psychiatric symptom clusters.

As an example of the increasing popularity of the structured group model, one can look at the types of circumstances in which these techniques have been used successfully: anxiety and mood disorders including social phobia (Barlow, 1994), residual depression (Fava et al., 1994), addictive behavior, parenting skills, anger control, shyness, incest survivors (McKay & Paleg, 1992), and many others. Fay and Lazarus (1993) described this nicely in their summary statement that, "Behavioral methods have been applied in groups to constellations of problem behaviors and skills deficits encompassed by various diagnostic categories such as the range of anxiety disorders, some mood disorders, eating disorders, substance abuse, stress management, couples and family communication problems, personality disorders including borderline and antisocial personalities, habit disorders, sexual dysfunction, paraphilias, and a variety of problems subsumed under the rubric of behavioral medicine, such as coronary prevention and pain management" (pp. 454–455).

Seligman and Marshak (1990) also compile a list of conditions for which psychotherapeutic groups can be particularly helpful. They include groups for patients with post-traumatic stress disorder, chronic problems with infertility, suicidal adolescents, agoraphobia, sexually abused children, Alzheimer's disease, and others. While their work is not exclusively concerned with the short-term group, it offers many thoughtful ideas that can be easily incorporated into technically eclectic brief group therapy models.

The majority of structured, time-limited groups are based on the principles of cognitive and behavioral therapies, both of which rely on learning theory as the foundation of the intervention model. In the cognitive/behavioral model, the theoretical underpinnings of the group techniques chosen are predicated on the assumption that maladaptive behavior and many psychological symptoms are learned and can be "unlearned," modified, alleviated, or eradicated through the application of a method that uses a systematic and symptom-specific cognitive/behavioral approach.

Basic to the model of the structured cognitive/behavioral group is a set of governing principles that determine the form and content of a given group. In short, these ideas are that: The presenting problems are taken at face value and are not seen as symptomatic of "deeper" psychopathology; the patient's current level of function and how his/her symptoms interfere with the harmonious conduct of life forms the basis for the intervention; language is used more in the service of symptom or behavioral description, while technical diagnostic labels are rarely used; the role of the therapist is a very active one in both structuring the group and leading each session with a specific therapeutic agenda; the therapist takes a high degree of responsibility for the outcome of the group; out-of-session behavioral assignments are a regular part of the group model; the therapist tries to be more of a scientist than a judge by trying to understand behavior and its meaning rather than apply value judgments to it; there is a strong emphasis on "self-management" in order to increase and reinforce autonomous behavior outside of group therapy; the patient's familial and social networks are valued and enlisted in trying to create a life situation that is maximally reinforcing to the gains made in the group.

The advantage of conducting the structured cognitive/behavioral approach in the group setting lies in the increased opportunities for learning, practicing, and refining newly acquired information. Role-playing, assertiveness exercises, and interpersonal experimentation with new attitudes or behaviors can be encouraged in the safety of the group setting. In essence, opportunities for learning are enhanced in all groups but are of special value to the group therapist who works with a cognitive/behavioral orientation.

A typical clinical example of this group model can be seen by taking a representative session plan from an established structured cognitive-behavioral group. The example chosen is from the Albany Social Phobia Protocol (Barlow, 1994). This is a 14-week program of which the outline for sessions three through 11 will be presented. Four central components comprise the heart of this middle phase of the group: Patients complete the Beck Depression Inventory and any other relevant testing or evaluation measures, homework from the previous session is reviewed, a therapeutic task is assigned to be carried out in the session, and homework for the next week is designed.

The third part of the session is the most illustrative part of what actually happens in the bulk of the group session. In this segment of the Albany protocol, the third part of the meeting for members working on their social phobic symptoms is specifically delineated as follows:

PART THREE OF SESSION THREE: ALBANY SOCIAL PHOBIA PROTOCOL (BARLOW, 1994, P. A49)

Complete three in-session exposures

    a. Select target group member and briefly outline exposure situation.

    b. Elicit automatic thoughts.

    c. Pick one or two thoughts to pursue further.

    d. Label cognitive distortion(s) in selected automatic thought(s).

    e. Challenge selected automatic thought(s) using the dispute handles.

    f. Develop one or two rational responses.

    g. Develop details of the exposure situations.

    h. Set a non-perfectionistic, behavioral goal.

    i. Complete role play.

    j. Debrief exposure.

        1. Review goal attainment.

        2. Carry out other activities as appropriate.

Structured groups have broad appeal, as one can see from the example above. The provider has a clear and systematic method for proceeding with therapy. Patient goals and methods for their completion are explicit but not rigid, and patients are not kept in the dark about what to expect in this kind of group therapy.

The implications for managed care are very important ones. Structured cognitive-behavioral groups are the clearest in describing what transpires in treatment. They employ methods that are reproducible and lend themselves to easy measurement of outcome. They are time-limited, yet still allow for flexibility within the fixed time frame. These groups are symptom and behaviorally focused, thereby lending themselves nicely to highly specific treatment plans. They concentrate on the patient's current level of functioning and conceptualize it in terms of behavior that can be modified through the use of a cost-efficient brief group therapy model.

The goals, methods, and language of these groups is very much in concert with the goals and language of managed mental health care. It will not be surprising to see a proliferation of similar group formats as long as managed care retains an interest in short-term, economical methods of psychological treatment.

This chapter has taken an overview of some "exceptions to the rule" in managed care. Patients, problems, and settings that call for innovation and departure from strict, fixed-time guidelines have been the focal point of discussion. It seems clear that providers under managed care and managed care systems themselves will have to come to terms concerning conventional theories and traditional treatments of psychiatric patients. Practitioners will have to expand their therapeutic range of skills and managed care will have to understand the rationale for some "special" situations that will simply not respond to guidelines created by economic as opposed to clinical standards.

Part IV

Documenting the Group Experience and Evaluating the Outcome

12

Recording and Reporting the Managed Care Group Experience

RECORDING THE GROUP EXPERIENCE

Responsible group therapists keep good records of the significant elements in their groups regardless of the context in which they are working. In the managed care context, regular record keeping simplifies the process of reporting clinical data and patient information to reviewing sources.

Different systems of managed care will have their own referral mechanism for getting the patient from initial evaluation to group placement. When the evaluator and group provider are one in the same, this simplifies the process of group referral enormously. In clinical settings where the evaluator is someone other than the group leader, as is the case in most outpatient clinic settings, it is very important to have a standardized system in place for insuring that the group referral process goes smoothly. Problems with inadequate, informal, or too loosely structured group referral procedures result in several serious but avoidable problems.

Most often, there is inadequate communication between the referring clinician and the group leader. At best, this results in a long waiting period for patients before they are actually assigned to a group. At worst, many patients are disappointed, feel neglected, and lose interest in being in group. The point of group referral is a time of high risk for patients to drop out of group therapy or get "lost" in the bureaucratic system.

This is a totally avoidable scenario. One solution is to have the group parallel of a "gatekeeper" in the managed care system. This is usually a clinician who is experienced in group work and serves as a coordinator of group services. The role entails identifying patients in the system who are good candidates for group, being available to clinicians for consultation if there is doubt about proper group placement, and tracking the referral process from initial screening to referral to group through actual patient entry into the group.

In terms of recording this process, two forms are utilized: a group therapy referral form (Exhibit 1) and a group therapy referral follow-up form (Exhibit 2). The referral form contains basic patient identification information, but also communicates a clear sense as to why this patient is being referred to group now. The form is designed in a way that both facilitates group referral and serves as guide for thinking about what will be needed to report to the managed care reviewer.

The group therapy referral follow-up form was created to provide a method of "checks and balances" in the overall managed care system to insure that no patient referred for group therapy gets "lost in the cracks" of the organization during this critical period. It serves the dual purpose of providing a written statement of the patient's clinical disposition and functioning as a feedback mechanism between group coordinator and group provider. This is very helpful in giving the provider a vehicle by which he/she can explain the rationale for declining to accept a patient into group. The group coordinator is informed immediately, by use of the form, so that an alternative and expeditious disposition plan can be made that more closely suits the needs of the patient.

Using these two forms together not only encourages smooth functioning of any managed care group treatment services but also "protects" the patient from unwarranted feelings of rejection when he/she is considered an unsuitable member for a particular group. The coordinator has instant access to the provider's clinical thought process and can immediately reengage the patient in the process of exploring other treatment options, which may often include recommendation for another type of group. The recording process continues in the evaluation phase and includes a working diagnosis and a set of initial, intermediate, and long-term goals for the patient. Some statement about the reasoning for opting to recommend a particular group for a given patient at this time and its relationship to the patient's overall treatment plan is a good starting point.

When formal group sessions begin, the issue of note taking becomes another aspect of recording the managed care group experience. Notes should be taken outside of sessions. There are several reasons for this preference. The taking of notes in group sessions often takes the therapist out of the flow of group interaction in a way that may appear to patients to be too distant, remote, disinterested, or uninvolved. While this can raise important individual and group dynamic issues, it is better for the therapist in the short-term group to be more actively involved in the group process.

It should be made clear that an active therapist posture does not mean that the therapist necessarily need be more verbal in style, nor does it preclude the emergence and examination of transferential issues in psychodynamic groups. It merely means that the therapist in a brief therapy group has to be "on the job" consistently and the taking of extensive notes in group meetings intrudes upon this function.

It has never been the practice of the author to take actual "process notes" in group. There is always much more that transpires in any session than can be captured in writing. Therapists who obsessively try to take verbatim notes in group meetings invariably fail to appreciate the nonverbal aspects of the group and are often seen by the group as rigid and perfectionistic. Therapists who are less experienced in groups and therapists who are anxious about leading groups often resort to the taking of copious notes as a defense against their own anxieties stimulated by the group situation.

The timing of recording notes about the group is best done as soon after the session as possible. An ideal time is, as MacKenzie's (1990) phrase implies, "while the experience and the sense of involvement are still alive" (p. 261).

The content of the notes written about group focus on two parameters: the course of the individual patient in the pursuit of his/her goals and the critical events in the transactions of the group itself. An example of a short note encapsulating both group and individual information is contained in the following vignette:

> Fred, a 44-year-old teacher, was referred to group for problems related to anxiety about speaking in public. This was his target goal for treatment. Fred opened the group today by discussing an upcoming presentation he had to make at work. This was the first time Fred initiated discussion in the group. Almost all members praised him for his "bravery" in putting forth his fears so quickly and clearly.

EXHIBIT 1
Group Therapy Referral Form

Patient's name: _____ *Case number:* _____

Home phone number: _____ *Work phone number:* _____

Age: _____ *Sex:* _____ *Referral source:* _____

Brief psychiatric history (include hospitalizations, type and extent of previous treatment, known stressors to symptom upsurge): _____
_____
_____

Current symptoms: _____
_____

Present social circumstances (include family situation, involvement with friends, family, and social/community networks): _____
_____
_____

Describe reason for referral to group therapy: _____
_____

What type of group do you recommend for this patient? _____
_____

What are the goals for this patient and how will group placement help implement them? _____
_____

Is group therapy to be primary modality or adjunctive? _____
Psychiatric diagnosis: _____
_____

Medical status: _____
_____

Current medications: _____
_____

Are there any scheduling problems (work, school, other therapies, etc.)?
_____

What is the patient's reaction to discussion of referral to group? _____
_____

Other information or considerations that might be important to patient's ability to participate or remain in group treatment. _____
_____
_____

EXHIBIT 2

Group Therapy Referral Follow-up Form

To: **Referral Source**
From: **Group Leader**
Re: **Patient 'X'**

____(A) We suggest your patient join the following group: (Name of group, leader's name, day, time, and place of meetings)

_____

_____

Please contact _____ (usually group leader's name and phone number) to arrange placement into group.

____(B) At this point in time we do not have an appropriate group for your patient but will place the patient on the waiting list and notify you as soon as a place is available.

____(C) We do not feel that this patient is suitable for our group at this time. (Please provide an explanation for this decision.)

_____

_____

_____

_____

_____

_____

_____

_____

_____

_____

_____

_____

For purposes of managed care reporting, notes about this patient should relate to his presenting problem and treatment goals. References to performance anxiety and shifts in that symptom over time are a central part of the patient's clinical record. Similar notations focused more on behavior change and less on diagnostic language help trace a patient's course through therapy and will be appreciated by case reviewers for the clarity it affords them in understanding the events in the therapeutic process to which they are not a direct witness.

From a practical point of view, the author finds it useful to make an individual note (similar to the one in the vignette above) in each member's chart and to keep a set of "group notes" that highlight the course of the whole group and serve as an aid for the provider in plotting a therapeutic agenda for future meetings.

Recording group phenomenology serves as a data bank for the therapist to refer to for a variety of purposes. Group notes should include a record of attendance, the major group theme or themes discussed in each session, any crisis situations, unexpected or unusual behaviors that arise, which members were active and which were withdrawn, and a plan for the next group session. A sample individual progress note for a patient in group (Exhibit 3) and a model for a "group note" (Exhibit 4) illustrate the form in which group information can be recorded.

If any formal individual or group testing is done initially or in ongoing sessions, this data should also be included in the progress notes. Examples touched upon earlier such as the patient's Global Assessment of Functioning, the Structural Analysis of Social Behavior, the Beck Depression Inventory, and the like would be the kind of information recorded in this section of the patient's record.

The final component of recording the managed care group experience takes place when the group is over. A group termination summary should be completed, essentially reviewing the therapy and identifying areas of future concern (Exhibit 5).

REPORTING THE GROUP EXPERIENCE

When the time comes to communicate with the managed care organization, the information contained in the group records forms the basis

EXHIBIT 3
Individual Progress Note Form

Patient	Group	Date of session

Working Diagnosis: *309.24-Adjustment Disorder with anxious mood*

Major Symptoms: *Social isolation, somatic complaints—sweating, "rapid" heart rate, stomach pains; avoidant behavior in fearful situations.*

In-Group Behavior (level of participation, prevailing mood, main interpersonal posture adopted in sessions, attitude and behavior toward the therapist): *John remains on the periphery of the group and contributes infrequently. When confronted directly by members or the leader, he tends to give monosyllabic responses and says he is afraid to "expose" himself to others.*

Individual Treatment Goals: *Work on interpersonal anxiety utilizing the support elements present in group. Gently encourage more active participation and self-disclosure by modeling this with other group members and by judicious use of therapist self-disclosure in selected areas.*

Progress Towards Goal Attainment: *John still remains aloof but seems to have developed the beginnings of a bond with the other male group members. He described taking the same bus home from group with Felix after last week's session.*

Treatment Plan: *Therapist will sit next to John to concretize issues of support. Next group meeting will be theme-focused in order to take the pressure off John and to help him participate in group discussions around a shared group issue. Possibility of antianxiety medication will be considered if his progress continues to be slow or if he shows signs of regressing to earlier withdrawn behavior.*

Prognosis (some informal estimate of patient's capacity for change based on group participation to date): *John appears to be "coming out of his shell" and if this trend continues it appears that the group will be of great value to him.*

EXHIBIT 4
Group Note Form

Group Leader   **Date**
Members Present   **Session #**

Group Goals (eg., Social skills training) _____

_____

Focus of Current Session (eg., Group discussed anxieties connected with meeting new people or being in unfamiliar situations) _____

_____

Any Specific Problems Impeding Group Progress (eg., Mr. L. mentioned that he was thinking of dropping out of the group) _____

_____

Major Interventions/Techniques (eg., Utilized group support and universalization to reassure Mr. L. and encouraged him to remain in group. Also did brief role-playing exercise addressed at learning techniques for how to manage when meeting new people) _____

_____

Plans for Next Session (eg., Try to get Mr. L. to begin the group discussion; discuss his reaction and those of the other group members to today's session. Assign "homework" outside of group in which each member has to introduce themselves to a new person or "stranger" and report the experience back to the group) _____

_____

Therapist Factors (eg., Co-therapy issues; practical matters such as leader vacation schedule; need for consultation/supervision about a specific leadership or membership problem) _____

_____

Any Changes in Group Composition (eg., Dropouts from group; addition of new members) _____

_____

Other Comments (eg., Notify the group about upcoming holiday and discuss the possibilities for changing the meeting to another day of the week in order not to lose the continuity of the sessions) _____

_____

EXHIBIT 5

Group Termination Summary

Patient: **Leader:**
Group: *Women's Bereavement Group*

Initial Diagnosis: 300.4–Dysthymic disorder

Final Diagnosis: 309.0–Adjustment disorder with depressed mood

Target Goals: 1. Assess suicidal tendencies.
2. Evaluate for antidepressant medication.
3. Consider group therapy to counter social isolation and encourage expression of affect surrounding loss.
4. Encourage patient to return to work when clinical condition permits.

Goals Met: 1. Patient not suicidal, only mildly depressed mood remains.
2. Patient did not require antidepressant medication.
3. After initial hesitancy, patient participated actively in group. Reported that she felt like she "already made some new friends" in the group.
4. Patient has resumed work on a part-time basis. Feels "fatigued" at the end of the work day.

Residual Issues: 1. Mildly depressed mood but no longer has obsessional preoccupation with death of mother.
2. Not yet back at full-time work.

Follow-up Plan: 1. Return for evaluation in three months.
2. Encourage socialization around church activities.
3. Patient knows warning signs of depression and agrees to call in if necessary for earlier appointment.

Prognosis: Good. Patient was very fearful but followed suggestions of therapist and group. Well liked by others. No prior history of depressive illness in patient or family.

Areas of Concern in the Future:
1. Observe for signs of recurrent mood disorder.
2. Make sure patient does not become interpersonally isolated.
3. Watch patient carefully in the event of any deaths in her family or friendship circle.

Other Comments: Patient did not have sufficient neurovegetative symptoms of depression to warrant a trial of antidepressant medication.

for a fruitful dialogue. Since it is certain that the provider will be asked to describe a patient's clinical course, it is useful to have the group notations on hand.

Managed care companies differ in the form and content they require for case review purposes so that is not possible to present a "universal" format for reporting the group. Since most companies evaluate treatment on a case-by-case, rather than group, basis, it is best to focus on the individual member of the group and supply the requested information in individual terms, using the patient's in-group behavior as the major basis for the report.

Case review can be conducted in response to a written form provided by the managed care company. These are self-explanatory and usually ask for details concerning diagnosis, chief complaint, problems to be treated, an estimate of the severity of the patient's symptoms, preferred method of treatment, adjunctive treatment measures, medications the patient may be taking, medical status, and an opinion about the expected duration of further treatment and the rationale for the answer given.

When the case review takes place on the telephone, it is advisable to discuss it in everyday language and in an organized fashion. One way of doing this is to follow the diagnosis with a description of the presenting problem, the relevant past history, and the current symptoms and behavior. Next, the provider will ordinarily be asked to discuss progress toward the treatment goals and objectives and the plan for implementation of same. When group therapy is indicated or already in progress, the provider should be prepared to outline several reasons for the choice of group treatment.

The following is an excerpt from a telephone case review conducted midway in the course of treatment of a 56-year-old, single woman who was experiencing symptoms of clinical depression following the death of her mother six months ago. The reviewer asked the provider to discuss the plan for placing this woman in a 10-session "widows" group.

The provider's response took the following form: "Group therapy was suggested because the patient had no immediate family in the area and felt there was no one with whom she could "talk about her mother." She needed an outlet for the expression of these feelings in an atmosphere where other people had experienced a similar loss. She said she feels better when she can "get things off my chest," but she felt a sense of "weirdness" in "imposing" on the few friends she had.

This particular group was chosen for her in the hopes of helping her to feel more comfortable in "opening up" about her grief and strengthening her sagging self-esteem through the support and empathic elements of the group .

The plan is also to utilize the communication and socialization skills learned in the group to better equip her to broaden her social network. When she began crying in session four, the group rose to her aid and helped her feel "more normal" and "less depressed." The educational elements in the group have taught her to distinguish between normal grief and "pathological" grief or depression.

Her sleep pattern has improved as has her general level of "interest in living." She said she still felt "a bit shaky" but she is no longer preoccupied with "morbid" thoughts that used to "paralyze me with fear." She has returned to her work on a part-time basis and has joined a local church and its associated book club.

Her plans for the immediate future include moving out of the home she and her mother had shared and taking an apartment on her own. She has opted, and I agree with her decision, to defer a decision about pursuing any further therapy for at least a three month period, at which time a follow-up appointment has been made.

Regardless of the form it takes, effective communication between provider and the managed care organization is a sine qua non of good outcome in treatment. Dialogue surrounding clinical, administrative, managerial, and economic issues helps to clarify issues for all concerned and makes a decided contribution to the smooth conduct of group therapy in the era of managed care.

13

Evaluating the Outcome in Brief Group Psychotherapy

For many years, the field of group psychotherapy labored under the unwarranted reputation of being highly subjective, impressionistic, and "unscientific." The basis for this claim resided in the fact that the literature on group treatment was filled with unsubstantiated theoretical constructs, clinical enthusiasm, and largely anecdotal reports of new applications of group therapy, but no corresponding research to support the descriptions of successful outcome in group experiences.

Over the past two decades, practitioners of group therapy have recognized their own need to better understand the inner workings of psychotherapy groups and to apply the standards of first-rate clinical research to delineate how groups work. This trend gave rise to many essential questions about psychotherapy groups and posed some critical problems for researchers in the field.

A sampling of the kinds of inquiry raised by group therapists, the scientific community, and the public sector included: Are there specific therapeutic methods that are reproducible rather than idiosyncratic and that can be studied by others to see if the same results emerge? What are the operative mechanisms through which groups result in being truly "therapeutic"? What are the risk factors associated with group work? How can the use of labor-intensive leadership variations such as co-therapy and team leadership be shown to be worth the expenditure of staff time? How can outcome be measured in a reliable way, given the complexity of group therapy in contrast to individual psychotherapy?

It is this last question that forms the basis for concern to the managed care industry and to clinicians alike. This chapter will cite some of the relevant work being done in the field of outcome studies of brief psychotherapy groups. Each author or study is presented to highlight some basic attempt to answer some of the questions raised above. There is no intent to conduct an encyclopedic review of the literature on outcome, but rather to provide the reader with a flavor of what is of concern to all involved with short-term groups and to provide a representative sampling of interesting and important approaches to the issue of clinical outcome.

When one reviews the general literature on outcome in all types of brief psychotherapy, it is immediately apparent that this is a young field. If the total field is in its youth, then that part of it addressing outcome on brief group psychotherapy is in its infancy, and the data referable to outcome in managed care groups is still "in utero." There is, however, a small but solid body of studies that evaluate time-limited groups in a managed care setting. This will provide the focal point for two subjects to be accented in this chapter: What are the findings of these studies and what are the problems encountered in trying to conduct research on brief group psychotherapy?

Many variables contribute to the success or failure of group therapy. Areas that are common sites for study referable to outcome in brief groups include group cohesion, leadership style, group composition, time factors, and measures of patient satisfaction with treatment. A number of authors have addressed these elements in time-limited groups and have made some thought-provoking observations that have called some widely accepted ideas into question.

Although the ultimate focus here is on the managed care group, the outcome studies currently emerging are based on a set of assumptions originating in the studies of brief psychotherapy in general. In order to put the findings of current research into any meaningful context, it is important to review some of these basic observations that form the foundation for many short-term psychotherapies.

MacKenzie (1990) uses some outcome data to support the use of group therapy not only on equal footing with individual psychotherapy, but as the treatment of choice in selected cases. "The outcome literature provides justification for greater use of group psychotherapy approaches. Groups appear to offer equal therapeutic outcome with greater efficiency" (pp. 226–227). An analysis of time factors and attendance patterns are two pieces of evidence used in support of this premise.

As he goes on to note, "in most outpatient programs, about two-thirds of the patients are seen for six sessions or less, and less than 10% attend for more than 25 sessions.... Quite consistently in outpatient samples, approximately 50% of patients showed improvement by the 8th session, and 75% by the 26th session" (p. 227). Whether in individual or group formats, the results are equivalent. In addition, independent of the method of data collection, therapist evaluation, patient self-ratings, or independent observer findings, the same findings are seen consistently.

Garfield and Bergin's (1986) research concerning the length of time spent in outpatient settings noted an average figure of approximately four to eight sessions. This figure does not distinguish among the types of psychotherapy employed, but corresponds nonetheless to the consensus in the general psychotherapy literature.

Statistically, the length of time spent in treatment varies to some degree with the problem set of the patient and the acuteness or chronicity of the symptoms. MacKenzie cites figures from the psychotherapy literature that conclude with the findings that, "the range of sessions for patients in crisis is usually about 6 sessions and for brief individual therapy is from 12-25 sessions" (p. 229). The analogous review of the literature on brief group psychotherapy has led him to state that it is usual to "see results of time-limited groups running from eight to about 40 sessions" (p. 229).

Piper, McCallum, and Azim (1992) did a study in which they found that an exploration of a patient's degree of "psychological mindedness" and the general level of object relations were correlated with outcome in brief psychotherapy groups. The patients with high scores on both scales did not appear to benefit from a structured group format, whereas those with the lower scores did poorly in groups that provided less structure and expected more spontaneous participation by members.

McCallum, Piper, and Morin (1993) studied the relationship of affect to outcome in short-term psychoanalytically oriented groups for patients who had experienced major losses in their lives. They looked at the "cathartic hypothesis" in psychotherapy that roughly equates the expression of affect with positive outcome. They found it useful to refine this concept further and to separate affect into positive and negative forms. The results of the study indicated that catharsis of negative affect (sadness, anger, guilt, fear) was most effective when it was "integrated with psychodynamic work" (p. 316). The expression of positive affect grew over the course of the group and was directly correlated with positive outcome.

Piper (1994) has also looked at patient or client variables as they relate to outcome in brief psychotherapy groups. He examined factors that included dyadic interview data, direct observation of client behavior in dyadic and group situations, psychological testing results, age, sex, educational and employment status, social status, formal psychiatric diagnosis, and expectancy of treatment variables. The conclusions reached in his studies have clinical relevance not only to outcome, but perhaps more importantly to factors in the group such as patient selection, group composition, and the foundations for interaction in groups, all of which have dramatic influence on treatment outcome.

While the study itself explores important group themes, it is included here as much for its structure and design as for its clinical implications. Piper's work represents a healthy marriage between serious research and clinical application of the findings. His work on patient matching in groups, the employment of psychodynamic principles in brief therapy groups, and the studies on patients who have experienced grief over losses typify a trend in contemporary group psychotherapy that is returning a high yield of soundly researched data.

Others have turned their attention to developing instruments for measuring different facets of group psychotherapy. Hamilton et al. (1993) have designed ways of developing "monitoring indicators" used in the analysis of the integration of group therapy into treatment planning and to assess the competence and techniques of group psychotherapists. Their work has practical implications for managed care as one of several systems being used as a method of quality control in group treatment.

The leadership role in brief therapy groups is a core group variable that has been studied. MacKenzie (1990) defined four aspects of leadership style and related them to outcome in time-limited psychotherapy groups. He categorized the following styles, "caring and support, cognitive understanding, therapist control, and stimulation of emotional arousal" (p. 199). Of these, caring and cognitive work have the most direct and beneficial effect on outcome in the group.

In the discussion of his findings, MacKenzie not only reveals the methods by which he came to these conclusions, but also provides an explanation of some of the deleterious factors related to negative outcome in brief groups. As an instance of this, he states that, "Groups with low levels of leader control become disorganized and lose their task focus. High levels of control have an inhibiting effect on group participation. Groups with low levels of leader stimulation tend to be flat and uninteresting to the members. High stimulation levels produced active and exciting groups, but also a higher number of casualties" (p. 199).

Budman and co-workers at the Harvard Community Health Plan have made an ongoing contribution to the understanding of brief psychotherapy. Starting with brief individual psychotherapy in the 1980s, they have moved into the study of brief group psychotherapy in more recent times. They, too, have made a number of important research-based observations about many aspects of the short-term group.

Their work includes information that has direct bearing on outcome in short-term groups, some of which will echo other studies cited above and some casting new light on old themes. A simple way to get an overview of their orientation is to look at how they view factors related to outcome in brief group psychotherapy.

Budman, Simeone, Reilly, and Demby (1994) summarized the brief group experience by dividing it into several of its component parts and commenting on each. Time factors are central to their work and they describe a relatively low dropout rate (16.6%) with the use of a planned 15-session group therapy program for adolescents. The groups in this study were led by experienced group therapists (Budman, Demby & Randall, 1980).

Time enters into their view of outcome in another significant way that requires some background information for one to fully appreciate the significance of their findings. Budman, Simeone, Reilly, and Demby regard short-term group experiences as, "often only one component of a more expansive (and often lifelong) process of change. This is an important point because it changes the way in which we think about measuring outcome in time-limited therapy in general. Rather than thinking about 'cure,' we are thinking about limited improvement and changes. Therapy goals then become more realistic and achievable" (p. 322).

This treatment philosophy is very much in keeping with Poey's (1985) notion of selecting group goals attainable within the brief time frame of the group. In order to accomplish this, one sees the focus, here too, on working in the present, dealing with manifest group behavior, taking a supportive therapeutic stance, using the leader as a positive role model, and assigning tasks to the group both in and outside of sessions.

Group cohesion is element felt to be, "a central factor contributing to positive outcome in group psychotherapy" (Budman et al., 1993). In order to reach a therapeutic state of group cohesion, Budman, like Piper and others, believes strongly in the value of pre-group preparation of patients entering the short-term group. Although most leaders of psychotherapy groups value group cohesion as a therapeutic factor, Budman points out that it is a very difficult subject to research and there is a sparseness of studies relating group cohesion to outcome in brief treatment.

The most succinct statement of the conclusions gleaned from the research and clinical experience of the Harvard group is contained in the following summary: "short-term group treatment is most effective when goals are limited and achievable, and time is viewed as catalytic rather than constraining. In general, the short-term group therapist must adopt a style which is active, supportive, and directive, all the while using homework, advice-giving, and extra-therapeutic resources as effective adjuncts to treatment. Transference work, while central to some short-term approaches, is generally de-emphasized as this is frequently regressive and counter progressive. In brief, short-term group treatment is found to be effective when these critical conditions are adequately and consistently achieved" (Budman et al., 1994).

This review of some of the highlights is intended as part of a guide for providers to accelerate their access to new information emerging from research and clinical investigation of the brief group therapy model. As Klein (1993), a leading figure in psychopharmacological research, has warned, there is a gap in the time that elapses between laboratory discovery and clinical application of the findings. As he states with respect to drug research, "Current knowledge is not regularly applied. It has been repeatedly shown that the majority of patients with psychiatric illness go undiagnosed, and even if diagnosed, they are inappropriately or ineffectively treated, both by clinical psychiatrists and by primary care practitioners. Improved care depends on practitioner education, often referred to as 'technology transfer'" (p. 491).

The goal of this chapter has been to help "point a way" for clinicians to have earlier access to rapidly emerging information about short-term therapy groups in order to reduce the "technology transfer" time in the psychotherapeutic sector of the field of mental health care.

14

Future Directions and New Challenges

Psychotherapy in the age of health care reform is under scrutiny, if not under siege. It is estimated that each year 80 million outpatient medical visits are made for the purposes of receiving psychotherapy (Olfson & Pincus, 1994a). It is an understatement to suggest that "the future of third-party reimbursement for long-term psychotherapy services rests on unstable ground" (Olfson & Pincus, 1994b). Psychotherapeutic interventions of brief models as well as of long-term models are being assessed for purposes of justifying their very existence as entities under a system of managed mental health care.

Thus far in this text, we have looked at the history and contemporary practice of brief group psychotherapy and of managed care. It is now time to turn attention away from the "rear view mirror" and look to the future. While there are innumerable areas making for interesting discussion, four representative areas of future concern will be singled out for exploration. In the true spirit of "time-effective" group therapy practice, an effort will be made to keep the discussion specific, focused, goal-directed, and brief. The four topics to be addressed are: (1) The role of standardized treatments for specific psychiatric conditions. (2) Ethical concerns produced by the changes in health care service delivery. (3) Future trends. (4) The implication of mental health care reform for the group therapy practitioner.

CLINICAL PRACTICE GUIDELINES

Recently, there has been a growing interest in standardizing the criteria for treatment of psychiatric patients in specific diagnostic categories. Two prominent examples of this are to be found in the American Psychiatric Association's publication of "Practice Guidelines for Major Depressive Disorder in Adults" (April, 1993) and "Practice Guidelines for the Treatment of Patients With Bipolar Disorder" (December, 1994). What are the ramifications of standardized treatment guidelines for the practice of psychotherapy in a managed care environment?

Rush (1993) envisions an impact on the primary care physician as being a hopeful one. He expresses the view that if the guidelines are adopted and put into practice with the depressed patient, it could result in six advantages for primary care practice: (1) more careful interviewing and use of self-report screening instruments; (2) an extended initial evaluation; (3) better patient education about depression; (4) "One to three well-conducted, time-limited treatment trials (either medication, formal psychotherapy, or a combination) will likely follow with more frequent visits (weekly) than is now the case and with more attention to dosage adjustment"; (5) a greater emphasis on studying the outcome of treatment; (6) a better sense of when to refer patients to specialists.

In order to develop clinically valuable guidelines, four areas need to be taken into account: (1) Has the relevant scientific database been reviewed and documented? (2) What will the mechanism for distribution to the clinician be so that the broadest population will be reached? (3) How will the monitoring process take place? (4) How will the impact of the treatment guidelines be assessed so that information gained from users of the system can be used to amend or augment the guidelines when necessary? (McIntyre, 1994).

Markowitz (1994) offers a model for trials of a standardized psychotherapeutic treatment of dysthymia in which he proposes that the therapeutic trials be time-limited, manual-based psychotherapy with an interpersonal focus. The treatment would be, as compared to other treatments, such as antidepressant medication, continued and maintained in order to prevent recurrent dysthymic episodes. Follow-up assessment would take place six months after the termination of treatment.

One of the practical reasons that clinicians are interested in treatment guidelines is related to the issue of trying to regain control over clinical decision making from the hands of managed care companies. There are other reasons for their interest as well. The advantages of using a standardized diagnostic system (DSM-IV), the need to reduce excessive costs of current systems of utilization review, the desire to delineate what would be considered inappropriate treatments, and the need to expand the base for clinical research referable to outcome. Standardization would also reduce some of the "annoyances" of a managed care system, including excessive time spent on the telephone and getting bogged down in paperwork required by present managed care standards.

The potential disadvantages of a systematized set of clinical guidelines are severalfold. Not all patients fit the diagnostic criteria that look good on paper but may not correspond to a given patient's clinical state. In the dysthymia treatment model, what happens when the patient has a significant anxiety component in addition to his or her condition? Is the diagnosis dysthymia with agitated features or generalized anxiety disorder with depressive features?

Secondly, even though the treatment protocol may be outstanding, there is still that group of patients who will not respond to the prescribed therapeutic plan. What provisions will be made for them? For these patients, and probably for most patients, the goal is to be consistent with a treatment orientation described by Frances (1994) as, "delivering standardized therapy in a flexible way." This model still allows for clinical judgment and creativity in therapy while adhering to the framework of a standardized set of clinical guidelines.

Third, if one examines the process by which standardized treatment guidelines are created, it is not always easy to get a consensus among the group setting the standards. Most therapists have a preferred therapeutic belief system concerning what constitutes effective therapy for their patients. It is important that issues of science, not politics, govern the process of formulating a set of practice guidelines.

Finally, in spite of nearly every set of published guidelines citing the disclaimer that they are not to be taken rigidly in "cookie mold" therapy, there is still the risk that some clinicians will use them not as guidelines but as gospel. Clinical guidelines are not intended to be used as either "the Bible" or a "cookbook." They are best viewed as summaries of the latest scientific data pooled into a form that has clinical value in the direct application of research findings to clinical care.

ETHICAL ISSUES

A host of ethical issues is attached to the current and future changes in mental health treatment. The subjects of patient privacy and patient-therapist confidentiality are high on the list of ethical dilemmas posed for consumers and providers in any system of managed care.

All practitioners in managed care contexts have to guard against falling into the trap of breaching confidentiality as the price one pays for being part of a better managed system. Cost containment threatens to change aspects of the fundamental relationship between patient and therapist, particularly in the area of trust. Administrative requirements set down by managed care companies, employee assistance programs, utilization review specialists, and employers all can intrude upon the conduct of psychotherapy. Therapists in a managed care system have to protect their patients by providing safeguards against unauthorized release of patient information and by making certain that the person requesting the data has the proper authority, training, and motive for so doing.

Conflicts of interest form another broad category of ethical concern under managed care. In daily practice, one can see many examples of clinical decisions being influenced by powerful forces tempting the provider to alter what he/she would normally consider the best course of action in a specific case. Speaking frankly and not euphemistically, money matters are often at the base of these decisions. When a patient will be denied further services if his/her improved clinical condition is described accurately, there is incentive for the provider to "pathologize" the patient when reporting to the case reviewer in order to extend the length of treatment and corresponding benefits.

The decision to place someone on psychotropic medication can also be a sticking point for ethical issues. Medication may be clinically indicated, but it will frequently shorten the time spent in psychotherapeutic treatment. The provider has to be clear on the decision to medicate or not in order to insure that whichever choice is made is done in the patient's, not the provider's, best interest. Unethical practices of medicating difficult or unpopular patients in order to spend less time with them or get them out of treatment quickly, as well as decisions by nonpsychiatric providers to not make a medication evaluation referral for fear of "losing the case" or because the provider "doesn't believe in medication" are infrequent but blatant abuses of the managed care system.

Many providers are learning that they are not being accepted into managed care panels. Others are notified that their practice patterns are being "profiled" and a decision about whether or not to retain them or refer patients to them will be forthcoming. Providers are usually unaware as to how this process works but most get the message that "briefer is better" and that noncompliance with this model threatens their economic security by not insuring a regular referral stream into their practices.

The issue of parity between provider and case reviewer is assuming problematic proportions in certain circles. In a managed care model, the decision about treatment comes from the reviewer not the provider. Many providers are asking, "Who are these case reviewers?" Providers have asked for the credentials of those reviewing and judging their work to make certain that the reviewer is at least as qualified as the provider to render treatment decisions.

The incentives to do shorter and shorter treatment raise the specter of premature decisions being made in instances that can range from poor clinical judgment to harmfulness or endangerment as a consequence. This ethical issue comes into play in dramatic form when the time comes to decide when to discharge a seriously ill psychiatric patient from the hospital. It has to be understood that, regardless of the prevailing system of care, there are critical clinical assessments which need to be made by competent clinicians for the "right" reasons, i.e., what is the adaptive capacity of the patient to function outside the hospital.

An analogous example occurs when a patient is "pushed" into group therapy before he or she is emotionally able to participate in group or to withstand the high level of affect present in many brief therapy groups. Group therapy can be misused as a "dumping ground" for patients who have not done well in other therapies or because group therapy is a less expensive form of psychotherapy than its individual counterpart.

Capitated systems of managed care also hold the potential for ethical problems. If, as in some capitated systems, a program is underfunded, then the economic and treatment pressure it was designed to relieve comes up in altered form. Instead of relieving the provider of any economic intrusions into what is felt to be optimum patient care, there is new pressure to treat patients within the confines of the present budget. This state does not differ very much from noncapitated systems where the economic and therapeutic concerns are primary.

Last, but certainly not least on the list of ethical concerns, is the potential for discriminatory practices under a system of third-party payment. Historically, it has been the poorest members of the mentally ill community who have fared the worst. The fear is that managed care will not solve this problem and that a preferential mental health service delivery system will emerge. Many concerned with mental health care reform are well aware of this phenomenon and are trying to design new systems that will be truly democratic in dispensing psychiatric treatment. The Report of the National Advisory Mental Health Council (1993) and an editorial by Sharfstein (1993) are examples of the readiness of many in the mental health field to be advocates for the people who have not had adequate access to quality psychiatric treatment.

FUTURE TRENDS

Even with the demise of the Clinton Health Care Reform proposal, health care reform is very much alive. While no one can predict exactly what form the future mental health care delivery systems will take, it seems certain that a revision of traditional models is inevitable.

Ironically, this statement applies equally to systems of managed care currently in place. Although cost effectiveness is a guiding principle of managed care, many managed care organizations are not run efficiently, the present system of utilization review has come under fire as being too costly and too imprecise, and there are people on both the business and clinical sides of the present system who are developing newer, more efficient models for the future.

If one examines some trends in the field, certain educated guesses can be made as to what the health care delivery system of the future will resemble. It appears, with the defeat of the Clinton plan, that more responsibility for decisions regarding funding of mental health care may go to the state level.

Utilization review as we know it will probably become obsolete and will be replaced, in part, by sophisticated computer-driven medical and mental health information systems.

The discontent on the part of providers with their loss of autonomy and their rejection from the ranks of the treatment decision makers will lead to a greater formation of independent practice associations composed of groups of clinicians who will self-manage and self-regulate their programs.

Funding for mental health services may move toward a capitated model under which groups of providers will be given back the responsibility for clinical and economic apportionment of treatment services.

Provider groups have started, and no doubt will continue, to encourage diversity of services within their own networks. This is the model of what is colloquially known as "one-stop shopping" for psychiatric services.

A prototypical provider group would include: a central point of service; a 24-hour on-call provider; established treatment guidelines for different conditions; internal mechanisms for quality control; measuring instruments for patient satisfaction; standardized record-keeping and audit procedures; a formal process for reviewing controversial cases; a provider feedback component; a mental health database system that can perform functions of pre- and recertification of treatment, tracking of patient progress, monitoring patient referrals, and credentialing of staff; a provision for hospitalization when indicated; a greater use of innovative alternatives to hospitalization; and a staff training program.

Payers and providers are in dispute about future proposals such as the American Medical Associations's Patient Protection Act or similar proposals whose aim is to, as Sharfstein says, "level the playing field so that patients and physicians (providers) have fair access and maximum choice" (pp. 1767–1768). Those who favor such proposals are aware of the potential hazards involved in corporatizing medical care and want to insure that patients and providers are not treated in a discriminatory fashion.

Vested interest groups have concerns about their future roles. Psychiatrists fear that they will no longer be allowed to practice psychotherapy, but instead will be involuntarily relegated to the position of diagnostician, medication dispenser, consultant, or case supervisor. Psychodynamically oriented psychotherapists are concerned that they, too, will be prevented from doing what they know best and feel is the best for their patients. Many practicing clinicians are unfamiliar with the use of brief individual, group, and family therapies and are anxious about how they will acquire these skills.

This is only a smattering of concerns for the future. Managed care is only a symptom of an enormous transition in the ways in which health care is delivered and paid for. It is likely to go through several incarnations before reaching some semblance of stability and acceptability in the public and private sectors. The result will be, hopefully, a transformed delivery system that manages care as well as it does economics.

IMPLICATIONS OF MENTAL HEALTH CARE REFORM FOR GROUP THERAPISTS

In 1994, the presidential address given at the American Group Psychotherapy Association's annual meeting was on the theme of the challenge of mental health reform for group psychotherapy. At one point in his speech, Dr. Roy MacKenzie told the audience, "We are entering the third age of group psychotherapy...driven by...more sober considerations of a scientific and economic nature" (pp. 425–426). He urged group therapists to, "be on our guard that group methods not be trivialized by inadequate time or the use of poorly trained clinicians. We must be designers, not simply defenders" (pp. 425–426).

Group therapy has stood the test of time. It has proven itself to be among the most adaptable of psychotherapeutic techniques, not only by surviving but by being innovative, flexible, and unthreatened by change. This rich tradition is being tested once again. The battleground this time is managed mental health care. The people at risk are the patients and the ideology at stake depends upon how much group therapists believe in and can document, what they know to be valid from years of clinical work and research efforts.

While the emphasis in contemporary health care is on saving money and saving time, groups have much more to offer than to serve as repositories in which large numbers of people can be seen at one time so that a smaller number of people can make a large financial profit.

Group therapy belongs in the forefront of mental health care reform. It has proven time and again that there is hardly a patient population, diagnostic entity, socioeconomic class, or educational end for which a constructive group experience cannot be created. Group therapists are being asked to show what they have to contribute to the changing health care conundrum. Group therapy has an enormous and invaluable role to play in this process.

The role for group therapy under any system of managed care is one of leadership. Group therapists are adept at leading groups of all kinds. The simple fact is that group psychotherapists have the most experience in the format emerging as one, if not the preferred, treatment of choice under the new managed care models. There will be much more to group therapy and managed care in the future than just conducting short-term groups. Group therapists have already established a National Registry of Certified Group Psychotherapists as a tangible demonstration of their ongoing commitment to clinical excellence and to establishing a mechanism for public accountability. The registry represents an effort to insure that those who present themselves as practitioners of group psychotherapy have the requisite background and training to justify their claims.

Now is a time when group therapists can move forward and demonstrate their unique abilities. They can train other professionals as well as deliver the highest quality of services to patients under any system of health care.

Appendix A *

AMERICAN GROUP PSYCHOTHERAPY
ASSOCIATION, INC.

GUIDELINES FOR ETHICS

INTRODUCTION

The American Group Psychotherapy Association is a professional multidisciplinary organization whose purpose is to: "provide a forum for the exchange of ideas among qualified professional persons interested in group psychotherapy and to publish and to make publications available on all subjects relating to group psychotherapy; to encourage the development of sound training programs in group psychotherapy for qualified mental health professionals; to encourage and promote research on group psychotherapy and to establish and maintain high standards of ethical, professional group psychotherapy practice."

Membership in the American Group Psychotherapy Association presumes strict adherence to standards of ethical practice. As a specialty organization, AGPA supports the ethical codes of the primary professional organizations to which our members belong. Providing guidelines for the ethical behavior of group psychotherapists serves to inform both the group psychotherapist and public of the American Group Psychotherapy Association's expectations in the practice of group psychotherapy.

GENERAL GUIDELINES

Ethics complaints about AGPA members will be directed to the primary professional organization of the members. AGPA's response as to

---

*Reprinted with permission from the American Group Psychotherapy Association.

185

sanctions will parallel that of the primary organization. For example, if the primary organization concludes that an individual's membership should be suspended for one year, AGPA will suspend membership for one year. Should an ethical complaint be received regarding a member of AGPA who does not belong to a primary professional organization, the complainant will be directed to the state licensing board and/or the state or federal legal system. If the member is found guilty, AGPA's sanctions will parallel the sanctions of the state licensing board, other governmental agencies or courts of law as to the person's ability to practice; the AGPA cannot parallel such sanctions as fines, penalties or imprisonment.

For those members of the American Group Psychotherapy Association who are psychiatrists, the principles of ethics as applied by the American Psychiatric Association shall govern their behavior; those members who are clinical psychologists shall be expected to comply with the principles of ethics laid down by the American Psychological Association; those members who are clinical social workers shall be expected to comply with the ethical standards established by the National Federation of Societies for Clinical Social Work; those members who are clinical specialists in nursing shall be expected to comply with the principles of ethics of the American Nurses' Association; those members who are pastoral counselors shall be expected to comply with the ethical standards of the American Association of Pastoral Care; and those members of other professional disciplines having published principles of ethics shall follow those principles. Members of the Association who do not belong to one of the above professional groups having a published standard of ethics shall follow the principles of ethics laid down by the American Psychological Association.

GUIDELINES OF GROUP PSYCHOTHERAPY PRACTICE

The following guidelines of group psychotherapy practice shall serve as models for group therapists' ethical behavior.

RESPONSIBILITY TO PATIENT/CLIENT

1. The group psychotherapist provides services with respect for the dignity and uniqueness of each patient/client as well as the rights and autonomy of the individual patient/client.

1.1 The group psychotherapist shall provide the potential group patient/client with information about the nature of group psychotherapy and apprise them of their risks, rights and obligations as members of a therapy group.

1.2 The group psychotherapist shall encourage the patient/client's participation in group psychotherapy only so long as it is appropriate to the patient/client's needs.

1.3 The group psychotherapist shall not practice or condone any form of discrimination on the basis of race, color, sex, sexual orientation, age, religion, national origin or physical handicap, except that this guideline shall not prohibit group therapy practice with population specific or problem specific groups.

2. The group psychotherapist safeguards the patient/client's right to privacy by judiciously protecting information of a confidential nature.

2.1 The group shall agree that the patient/client as well as the psychotherapist shall protect the identity of its members.

2.2 The group psychotherapist shall not use identifiable information about the group or its members for teaching purposes, publication or professional presentations unless permission has been obtained and all measures have been taken to preserve patient/client anonymity.

2.3 Except where required by law, the group psychotherapist shall share information about the group members to others only after obtaining appropriate patient/client consent. Specific permission must be requested to permit conferring with the referring therapist or with the individual therapist where the patient/client is in conjoint therapy.

2.4 When clinical examination suggests that a patient/client may be dangerous to himself/herself or others, it is the group psychotherapist's ethical and legal obligation to take appropriate steps in order to be responsible to society in general, as well as, the patient/client.

3. The group psychotherapist acts to safeguard the patient/client and the public from the incompetent, unethical, illegal practice of any group psychotherapist.

3.1 The group psychotherapist must be aware of her/his own individual competencies, and when the needs of the patient/client are beyond the competencies of the psychotherapist, consultation must be sought from other qualified professionals or other appropriate sources.

3.2 The group psychotherapist shall not use her/his professional relationship to advance personal or business interests.

3.3 Sexual intimacy with patients/clients is unethical.

3.4 The group psychotherapist shall protect the patient/client and the public from misinformation and misrepresentation. She/he shall not use false or misleading advertising regarding her/his qualifications or skills as a group psychotherapist.

PROFESSIONAL STANDARDS

The group psychotherapist shall maintain the integrity of the practice of group psychotherapy.

1. It is the personal responsibility of the group psychotherapist to maintain competence in the practice of group psychotherapy through formal educational activities and informal learning experiences.

2. The group psychotherapist has a responsibility to contribute to the ongoing development of the body of knowledge pertaining to group psychotherapy whether involved as an investigator, participant, or user of research results.

3. The group psychotherapist shall accept the obligation to attempt to inform and alert other group psychotherapists who are violating ethical principles or to bring those violations to the attention of appropriate professional authorities.

(Revised February, 1991)

*Appendix B**

NATIONAL REGISTRY OF CERTIFIED
GROUP PSYCHOTHERAPISTS

INSTRUCTION GUIDELINES FOR COMPLETING
ELIGIBILITY FORM

Grandparenting Period:
January 1994–February 1996

The information provided on the Eligibility Form and the accompanying Supervision Verification Reference Forms and Group Psychotherapy Colleague Reference Forms will be used to determine your eligibility for inclusion in the National Registry of Certified Group Psychotherapists. Please read these instructions carefully *before* completing the application and please type or print.

ELIGIBILITY REQUIREMENTS

Registry eligibility requires both general clinical credentials and specific group psychotherapy credentials.

Clinical credentials include a graduate degree and state clinical licensure and/or clinical membership/certification in designated national professional organizations.

Group psychotherapy credentials include group psychotherapy education, experience, supervision, and references.

---

*Reprinted with permission from the National Registry of Certified Group Psychotherapists.

189

A. Clinical Credentials: This section establishes your credentials as a clinician.

1. Identifying Information

   Name must be listed as it appears on your license or membership/certification.

2. Education

   List all graduate degrees. A minimum of a Master's degree in a clinical mental health field or related health field is required.

   If you are a physician, please complete information on your residence training program in psychiatry.

3. Clinical Discipline

   If you have advanced degrees in more than one discipline, please list the primary one for which you are licensed or certified to practice as a clinical mental health professional in your state.

4. State Licensure

   Most states now regulate clinical practice with licensure. *You must have the highest level license available for your discipline in your state.* **A copy of your current license must accompany this application.**

5. Membership/Certification in National Professional Organizations

   This section is only for use by applicants for whom discipline licensure is not available, except for nurses who must also complete this section.

   If licensure is not available in your state or if you reside outside of the United States, membership or certification at the highest clinical level in designated national professional organizations may be used to verify credentials as a clinical mental health professional for the purposes of this Registry. **Proof of your clinical membership/certification must accompany this application.**

B. Group Psychotherapy Credentials

1. Group Psychotherapy Education: *Refer to Section C for Grandparenting Period waivers.*

   Required: Completion of a 12 hour course of study in group psychotherapy theory and practice.

2. Group Psychotherapy Experience: *Refer to Section C for Grandparenting Period waivers.*

   Required: 300 hours of group psychotherapy experience as a leader or co-leader accrued during or following clinical graduate training.

   Definition: To qualify as **group psychotherapy experience,** the groups must be clearly for the purpose of providing psychotherapy services to designated client/patient populations, that is that the client/patient must be receiving psychotherapy for valid mental disorders listed in DSM-III-R. Family therapy (unless multi-family groups), peer groups, self-help groups, training groups, and any groups that are not clearly designated to provide psychotherapy services to designated clients/patients do not qualify. Please list only those groups that meet the above definition.

   As hours are a determinant, please list carefully the dates groups began and ended and the hours accumulated for each group. For ongoing groups, write "ongoing" with today's date in lieu of the ending date. Only 300 hours of group psychotherapy experience must be listed, not all groups in which you have been a leader or co-leader.

3. Group Psychotherapy Supervision

   a. **Supervision: Requirements and Definition.**
   Refer to Section C for Grandparenting Period waivers.

   Required: 75 hours of group psychotherapy supervision accrued during or following clinical graduate training.

   Definition: To qualify as **group psychotherapy supervision,** such supervision must have occurred with an approved group psychotherapy supervisor in either an individual or group format and must have involved the regular presentation of group psychotherapy clinical material.

As supervision hours are a determinant, please list carefully the dates such supervision began and ended and the hours accumulated for each supervision experience. Only 75 hours of group psychotherapy supervision must be listed.

b. **Approved Group Psychotherapy Supervisor: Requirements and Definition.** *Refer to Section C for Grandparenting Period waivers.*

Required: All group psychotherapy supervisors who are listed under the 75 hour group psychotherapy supervision requirement must fill out a Supervisor Verification Reference Form with the exception of the specific situations listed under Section B4.

Definition: To qualify as an **approved group psychotherapy supervisor,** the supervisor must be a group psychotherapist who is listed, or is eligible for listing, in the National Registry of Certified Group Psychotherapists and who has a total of 600 hours of group psychotherapy experience. This requires an additional 300 hours beyond Registry eligibility standards. Verification of supervisor qualifications will be affirmed by supervisor signature on the Supervision Verification Reference Form.

4. Group Psychotherapy Reference Forms: *Refer to Section C for Grandparenting Period waivers.*

Required: All applicants must submit a minimum of two completed reference forms with the application.

The Registry will use two types of reference forms to meet this requirement: the Supervision Verification Reference Form and the Group Psychotherapy Colleague Reference Form. **Supervision Verification Reference Forms** are completed by applicant's group psychotherapy supervisors. **Group Psychotherapy Colleague Reference Forms** are completed by colleagues who are practicing group psychotherapists who are familiar with applicant's group psychotherapy skills. Please note that family members may not be used on either type of reference form.

Applicants are required to submit completed **Supervision Verification Reference Forms** for all supervision used to meet the 75 hour group psychotherapy supervision requirement with the following exceptions:

In those cases where a single group psychotherapy supervisor has provided the 75 hours of group psychotherapy supervision, applicant may substitute a **Group Psychotherapy Colleague Reference Form** for the second reference.

In those cases where applicant cannot locate one or both supervisors, **Group Psychotherapy Colleague Reference Forms** may be substituted provided applicant states, on the Eligibility Form, the reasons supervisor(s) is not reachable.

References

Ackerman, N. W. (1958). *The Psychodynamics of Family Life.* Basic Books, New York.

Alexander, F., & French, J. M. (1974). *Psychoanalytic Therapy: Principles and Applications* [Reprint]. University of Nebraska Press, Lincoln, Nebraska. (Originally published in 1946).

Allport, G. (1948). Introduction. In K. Lewin, *Resolving Social Conflicts: Selected Papers on Group Dynamics.* Harper & Row, New York, p. vii.

American Psychiatric Association. (1993). Practice guidelines for major depressive disorder in adults. *American Journal of Psychiatry (supplement), 150*:1–26.

American Psychiatric Association. (1994). *Diagnostic and Statistical Manual of Mental Disorders, Fourth Edition.* American Psychiatric Association, Washington, DC.

American Psychiatric Association. (1994). Practice guidelines for the treatment of patients with bipolar disorder. *American Journal of Psychiatry (supplement), 151*:1–36.

American Psychiatric Association Committee on Managed Care. (1992). *Utilization Management: A Handbook for Psychiatrists.* American Psychiatric Association, Washington, DC.

Barlow, D. H. (1994). Comorbidity in social phobia: Implications for cognitive-behavioral treatment. *Bulletin of the Menninger Clinic (supplement A), 58*:A43–A57.

Beck, A. T., Rush, A. J., Shaw, B. F., & Emery, G. (1979). *Cognitive Therapy of Depression.* Guilford Press, New York.

Bennett, M. J. (1992). The managed care setting as a framework for clinical practice, In J. L. Feldman, & R. J. Fitzpatrick (Eds.), *Managed Mental Health Care.* American Psychiatric Press, Washington, DC, pp. 203–217.

Bernard, H. S. (1989). Guidelines to minimize premature terminations. *International Journal of Group Psychotherapy, 39*:523–529.

Bloom, B. L. (1992). *Planned Short-Term Psychotherapy.* Allyn & Bacon, Needham Heights, MA.

Budman, S. H. (1981). *Forms of Brief Therapy.* Guilford Press, New York.

Budman, S. H. (1992). Models of brief individual and group psychotherapy. In J. L. Feldman & R. J. Fitzpatrick (Eds.), *Managed Mental Health Care.* American Psychiatric Press, Washington, DC, pp. 231–248.

Budman, S. H., & Bennett, M. J. (1983). Short-term group psychotherapy. In H. I. Kaplan, & B. J. Sadock (Eds.), *Comprehensive Group Psychotherapy.* Williams & Wilkins, Baltimore, MD, pp. 138–144.

Budman, S. H., Demby, A., & Randall, M. (1980). Short-term group psychotherapy: Who succeeds, who fails? *Group, 4*:3–16.

Budman, S. H., & Gurman, A. S. (1988). *Theory and Practice of Brief Therapy.* Guilford Press, New York.

Budman, S. H., Simeone, P. G., Reilly R., & Demby, A., (1994). Progress in short-term and time-limited group psychotherapy: Evidence and implications. In A. Fuhriman, & G. M. Burlingame (Eds.), *Handbook of Group Psychotherapy.* John Wiley & Sons, New York, pp. 319–339.

Budman, S. H. et al. (1993). What is cohesiveness? An empirical examination. *Small Group Research, 24*:199–216.

Burlingame, G. M., & Fuhriman, A. (1990). Time-limited group therapy. *The Counseling Psychologist, 18*:93–118

Davanloo, H. (Ed.) (1980). *Short-term Dynamic Psychotherapy.* Jason Aronson, New York.

Dies, R. R., (1994). The therapists's role in group treatment. In H. S. Bernard & K. R. MacKenzie (Eds.), *Basics of Group Psychotherapy.* Guilford Press, New York, pp. 93–96.

Dies, R. R., & MacKenzie, K. R. (Eds.) (1983). *Advances in Group Psychotherapy: Integrating Research and Practice* (A.G.P.A. Monograph #1). International Universities Press, New York.

Dorwart, R. A. (1994). Healthcare reform: Reformation of practice? *Psychiatric Times,* March, p. 43.

Drob, S., & Bernard, H. S., (1986). Time-limited group treatment of genital herpes patients. *International Journal of Group Psychotherapy, 36*:133–144.

Fava, G. A. et al., (1994). Cognitive behavioral treatment of residual symptoms in primary major depressive disorder. *American Journal of Psychiatry, 151*:1295–1299.

Fay, A., & Lazarus, A. A. (1993). Cognitive-behavior group therapy. In A. Alonso, & H. I. Swiller, (Eds.), *Group Therapy in Clinical Practice.* American Psychiatric Press, Washington, DC, pp. 449–469.

Feldman, J. L., & Fitzpatrick, R. L. (Eds.) (1992). *Managed Mental Health Care: Administrative and Clinical Issues.* American Psychiatric Press, Washington, DC.

Forester, B., Kornfeld, D. S., Fleiss, J. L., & Thompson, S. (1993). Group psychotherapy during radiotherapy: Effects on emotional and physical distress. *American Journal of Psychiatry, 150*:1700–1706.

Frances, A. J. (1994). "How have the DSM and treatment guidelines changed psychiatrists' practice patterns?" Symposium #12, American Psychiatric Association Annual Meeting, Philadelphia, PA.

Frank, J. D. (1973). *Persuasion and Healing,* Revised edition. Johns Hopkins University Press, Baltimore, MD.

Freud, S. (1921). *Group Psychology and the Analysis of the Ego,* In *Standard Edition of the Complete Psychological Works of Sigmund Freud,* Vol. 18. Hogarth Press, London.

Friedman, W. H. (1989). *Practical Group Psychotherapy.* Jossey-Bass, San Francisco, CA.

Garfield, S. L., & Bergin, A. E. (Eds.) (1986). *Handbook of Psychotherapy and Behavior Change,* Third edition. John Wiley & Sons, New York.

Goodman, M., Brown, J., & Deitz, P. (1992). *Managing Managed Care: A Mental Health Practitioner's Survival Guide.* American Psychiatric Press, Washington, DC.

Grinker, R. R., & Spiegel, J. P. (1944). Brief psychotherapy in war neuroses. *Psychosomatic Medicine, 6*:123–131.

Gustafson, J. P. (1986). *The Complex Secret of Brief Psychotherapy.* W. W. Norton, New York.

Hamilton, J. D. et al. (1993). Quality assessment and improvement in group psychotherapy. *American Journal of Psychiatry, 150*:316–320.

Horwitz, L. (1977). Group psychotherapy of the borderline patient. In P. Hartocollis (Ed.), *Borderline Personality Disorders.* International Universities Press, New York.

Kanas, N. (1993). Group psychotherapy with bipolar patients: A review and synthesis. *International Journal of Group Psychotherapy, 43*:321–333.

Kelly, J. A., et al. (1993). Outcome of cognitive-behavioral and support group brief therapies for depressed, HIV-infected persons. *American Journal of Psychiatry, 150*: 1679–1686.

Kibel, H. D. (1980). The importance of a comprehensive clinical diagnosis for group psychotherapy of borderline and narcissistic patients. *International Journal of Group Psychotherapy, 304*:27–440.

Kibel, H. D. (1993a). Inpatient group psychotherapy. In A. Alonso & H. I. Swiller (Eds.), *Group Therapy in Clinical Practice.* American Psychiatric Press, Washington, DC, pp. 93–112.

Kibel, H. D. (1993b). Group psychotherapy. In E. Liebenluft, A. Tasman, & S. A. Green (Eds.), *Less Time to Do More: Psychotherapy on the Short-term Inpatient Unit.* American Psychiatric Press, Washington, DC.

Klein, D. F. (1993). Clinical psychopharmacologic practice: The need for developing a research base. *Archives of General Psychiatry, 50*:491–494.

Klein, R. H. (1985). Some principles of short-term group therapy. *International Journal of Group Psychotherapy, 35*:309–329.

Klerman, G. L., Weissman, M. M., Rounsaville, B. J., & Chevron, E. S. (1984). *Interpersonal Psychotherapy of Depression,* Basic Books, New York.

Lazell, E. W. (1921). The group treatment of dementia praecox. *Psychoanalytic Review, 8*:168.

Lewin, K. (1951). *Field Theory in Social Science.* Harper & Row, New York.

Lieberman, M. A., Yalom, I. D., & Miles, M. (1973). *Encounter Groups: First Facts.* Basic Books, New York.

Lindemann, E. (1944). Symptamatology and management of acute grief. *American Journal of Psychiatry, 101*:141–148.

Macaskill, N. (1982). Therapeutic factors in group therapy with borderline patients. *International Journal of Group Psychotherapy, 32*:61–74.

MacKenzie, K. R. (1990). *Introduction to Time-Limited Group Psychotherapy.* American Psychiatric Press, Washington, DC.

MacKenzie, K. R. (1993). Time-limited group theory and technique. In A. Alonso & H. I. Swiller (Eds.), *Group Therapy in Clinical Practice.* American Psychiatric Press, Washington, DC, pp. 423–447.

MacKenzie, K. R. (1994). Where is here and when is now? The adaptational challenge of mental health reform for group psychotherapy. *International Journal of Group Psychotherapy, 44*:407–428.

Malan, D. H. (1976). *The Frontier of Brief Psychotherapy.* Plenum Press, New York.

Mann, J. (1973). *Time-limited Psychotherapy.* Harvard University Press, Cambridge, MA.

Marcovitz, R. J., & Smith, J. E. (1983). An approach to time-limited dynamic inpatient group therapy. *Small Group Behavior, 14*:369–376.

Markowitz, J. C. (1994). Psychotherapy of dysthymia. *American Journal of Psychiatry, 151*:1114–1121.

Marsh, L. C. (1931). Group treatment of psychoses by the psychological equivalent of the revival. *Mental Hygiene, 15*:328.

Marziali, E., & Munroe-Blum, H. (1994). *Interpersonal Group Psychotherapy for Borderline Personality Disorder.* Basic Books, New York.

McCallum, M., Piper, W. E., & Morin H. (1993). Affect and outcome in short-term group therapy for loss. *International Journal of Group Psychotherapy, 43*: 303–319.

McCaughey, E. (1993). Health plan's devilish details. *Psychiatric Times*, November, pp. 12–13.

McIntyre, J. S. (1994). Practice guidelines. *Psychiatric Times*, August, pp. 22–23.

McKay, M., & Paleg, K. (Eds.) (1992). *Focal Group Psychotherapy*. New Harbinger, Oakland, CA.

Moreno, J. L. (1958). Fundamental rules and techniques of psychodrama. In J. H. Masserman & J. L. Moreno (Eds.), *Progress in Psychotherapy*. Grune & Stratton, New York.

Olfson, M., & Pincus, H. A. (1994a). Outpatient psychotherapy in the United States, I: Volume, costs and user characteristics. *American Journal of Psychiatry, 151*: 1281–1288.

Olfson, M., & Pincus, H. A., (1994b). Outpatient psychotherapy in the United States, II: Patterns of utilization. *American Journal of Psychiatry, 151*:1289–1294.

Pardes, H., & Pincus, H. A. (1981). Brief therapy in the context of national mental health issues. In S. H. Budman (Ed.), *Forms of Brief Therapy*. Guilford Press, New York, pp. 7–22.

Piper, W. E. (1994). Client variables. In A. Fuhriman & G. M. Burlingame (Eds.), *Handbook of Group Psychotherapy*. Wiley Interscience, New York, pp. 83–113.

Piper, W. E., Debanne, G., & Bienvenu, J. P. (1982). A study of group pre-training for group psychotherapy. *International Journal of Group Psychotherapy, 32*:309–325.

Piper, W. E., & Marrache, M. (1981). Pretraining for group therapy as a method of patient selection. *Small Group Behavior, 12*:459–475.

Piper, W. E., McCallum, M., & Azim, H. F. A. (1992). *Adaptation to Loss through Short-term Group Psychotherapy*. Guilford Press, New York.

Poey, K. (1985). Guidelines for the practice of brief, dynamic group therapy. *International Journal of Group Psychotherapy, 35*:331–354.

Pratt, J. H. (1907). The class method of treating consumption in the homes of the poor. *Journal of the American Medical Association, 49*:755–759.

Preferred Health Care Ltd. (1990). *The PHC Manual: Clinical Procedures and Protocols*. Wilton, CT.

Report of the National Advisory Mental Health Council (1993). *American Journal of Psychiatry, 150*:1445–1464.

Rice, A. R. (1995). Structured groups for the treatment of depression. In K. R. Mac Kenzie (Ed.), *Effective Use of Group Therapy in Managed Care*. American Psychiatric Press, Washington, DC, pp. 61–96.

Rice, C. A., & Rutan, J. S. (1987). *Inpatient Group Psychotherapy: A Psychodynamic Perspective*. Macmillan, New York.

Rodenhauser, P. (1989). Group psychotherapy and pharmacotherapy: Psychodynamic considerations. *International Journal of Group Psychotherapy, 39*:445–456.

Roth, B. (1982). Six types of borderline and narcissistic patients: An initial typology. *International Journal of Group Psychotherapy, 32*:9–27.

Rush, A. J. (1993). Clinical practice guidelines: Good news, bad news, or no news? *Archives of General Psychiatry, 50*:483–490.

Rutan, J. S., & Alonso, A. (1979). Group therapy. In A. Lazare (Ed.), *Out-patient Psychiatry: Diagnosis and Treatment*. Williams & Wilkins, Baltimore, MD.

Rutan, J. S., & Stone, W. N. (1984). *Psychodynamic Group Psychotherapy*. D.C. Heath, Lexington, MA.

Rutan, J. S., & Stone, W. N. (1993). *Psychodynamic Group Psychotherapy*, Second edition. Guilford Press, New York.

Sabin, J. E. (1981). Short-term group psychotherapy: Historical antecedents. In S. H. Budman (Ed.), *Forms of Brief Therapy*. Guilford Press, New York.

Segal, B. M., & Weideman, R. (1995). Outpatient groups for patients with personality disorders. In K. R. MacKenzie (Ed.), *Effective Use of Group Therapy in Managed Care*. American Psychiatric Press, Washington, DC, pp. 147–164.

Seligman, M., & Marshak, L. L. (Eds.) (1990). *Group Psychotherapy: Interventions with Special Populations*. Allyn & Bacon, Needham Heights, MA.

Sharfstein, S. S. (1993). Quality improvement. *American Journal of Psychiatry, 150*: 1767–1768.

Sifneos, P. E. (1992). *Short-Term Anxiety-Provoking Psychotherapy: A Treatment Manual*. Basic Books, New York.

Spiegel, D., & Yalom, I. D. (1978). A support group for dying patients. *International Journal of Group Psychotherapy, 28*:233–245.

Spitz, H. I. (1984). Contemporary trends in group psychotherapy: A literature survey. *Hospital and Community Psychiatry, 35*:132–142.

Spitz, H. I. (1987). Cocaine abuse: Therapeutic group approaches. In H. I. Spitz & J. R. Rosecan (Eds.), *Cocaine Abuse: New Directions in Treatment and Research*. Brunner/Mazel, New York, pp. 156–201.

Spitz, H. I., Kass, F., & Charles, E. (1980). Common mistakes made in group psychotherapy by beginning therapists. *American Journal of Psychiatry, 137*:1619–1621.

Stone, W., & Gustafson, J. (1982). Technique in group psychotherapy of narcissistic and borderline patients. *International Journal of Group Psychotherapy, 32*:29–48.

Winegar, N. (1992). *The Clinician's Guide to Managed Mental Health Care*. Haworth Press, New York.

Wong, N. (1980a). Focal issues in group psychotherapy of borderline and narcissistic patients. In L. R. Wolberg & M. L. Aronson (Eds.), *Group and Family Therapy:1980*. Brunner/Mazel, New York.

Wong, N. (1980b). Combined group and individual treatments of borderline and narcissistic patients: Heterogeneous versus homogeneous groups. *International Journal of Group Psychotherapy, 30*:389–404.

Yalom, I. D. (1975). *The Theory and Practice of Group Psychotherapy*. First edition. Basic Books, New York.

Yalom, I. D. (1983). *Inpatient Group Psychotherapy*. Basic Books, New York.

Yalom, I. D. (1985). *The Theory and Practice of Group Psychotherapy*, Third edition. Basic Books, New York.

Zaslav, M. R., & Kalb, R. D. (1989). Medicine as metaphor and medium in group psychotherapy with psychiatric patients. *International Journal of Group Psychotherapy, 39*:457–468.

Name Index

Ackerman, N. W., 20
Alexander, F., 16–17
Allport, G., 20
Alonso, A., 52–53
American Psychiatric Association, 7, 24, 31, 177
American Psychiatric Association Committee on Managed Care, 31, 35
Azim, H. F. A., 55, 77, 90–91, 172

Barlow, D. H., 153, 154–155
Beck, A. T., 17
Bellak, 17
Bennett, M. J., 99, 100
Bergin, A. E., 172
Bernard, H. S., 54–55, 62, 63
Bienvenu, J. P., 62, 69
Bloom, B. L., 17, 22, 25, 47
Brown, J., 5, 6, 36, 97–98
Budman, S. H., 17, 21, 23, 25, 91–93, 174, 175
Burlingame, G. M., 27

Charles, E., 64
Chevron, E. S., 17, 47, 48

Davanloo, H., 17, 47
Debanne, G., 62, 69

Deitz, P., 5, 6, 97–98
Demby, A., 174, 175
Dies, R. R., 131
Dorwart, R. A., 13
Drob, S., 54–55

Fava, G. A., 153
Fay, A., 153
Feldman, J. L., 5
Ferenczi, 16
Fitzpatrick, R. L., 5
Fleiss, J. L., 146
Forester, B., 146
Frances, A. J., 178
Frank, J. D., 117
French, J. M., 16–17
Freud, S., 16, 20
Friedman, W. H., 52, 53
Fuhriman, A., 27

Garfield, S. L., 172
Goodman, M., 5, 6, 36, 97–98
Grinker, R. R., 16
Gurman, A. S., 17, 23, 25, 91–93
Gustafson, J., 47, 149

Hamilton, J. D., 173
Horwitz, L., 149, 150

Kalb, R. D., 145
Kanas, N., 145
Kass, F., 64
Kelly, J. A., 146
Kibel, H. D., 140, 144, 149
Klein, D. F., 175
Klein, R. H., 27, 62
Klerman, G. L., 17, 47, 48
Kornfeld, D. S., 146

Lazarus, A. A., 153
Lazell, E. W., 20
Lewin, K., 20
Lieberman, M. A., 21

Macaskill, N., 149-150
MacKenzie, K. R., 21, 25-26, 27, 50,
    55, 68, 89, 122, 163, 171-172,
    173-174, 183
Malan, D. H., 17, 117
Mann, J., 47, 117
Marcovitz, R. J., 62
Markowitz, J. C., 177
Marrache, M., 69
Marsh, L. C., 20
Marshak, L. L., 153
Marziali, E., 149-150, 151-152
McCallum, M., 55, 77, 90-91, 172-173
McCaughey, E., 12
McIntyre, J. S., 177
McKay, M., 26, 61, 65, 153
Miles, M., 21
Moreno, J. L., 20
Morin, 172-173
Munroe-Blum, H., 150, 151-152

Olfson, M., 176

Paleg, K., 26, 61, 65, 153
Pardes, H., 22
Pincus, H. A., 22, 176
Piper, W. E., 55, 62, 69, 77, 90-91, 134,
    172-173, 173, 175
Poey, K., 54, 174

Pratt, J., 17, 20
Preferred Health Care Ltd., 31
Psychiatric News, 6, 8

Randall, M., 174
Rank, O., 16
Reilly, R., 174, 175
Report of the National Advisory Mental
    Health Council, 6, 181
Rice, A. R., 135-136
Rice, C. A., 140-142
Rodenhauser, P., 145
Rosecan, J. R., 18, 71
Roth, B., 149
Rounsaville, B. J., 17, 47, 48
Rush, A. J., 177
Rutan, J. S., 52-53, 134, 140-142

Sabin, J. E., 20, 117
Segal, B. M., 149-150, 151
Seligman, M., 153
Sharfstein, S. S., 181, 182
Sifneos, P. E., 17, 46-47, 117
Simeone, P. G., 174, 175
Smith, J. E., 62
Spiegel, D., 148
Spiegel, J. P., 16
Spitz, H. I., 18, 64, 69, 71, 86, 146
Stone, W., 149
Stone, W. N., 52-53, 134

Thompson, S., 146

Weideman, R., 149-150, 151
Weissman, M. M., 17, 47, 48
Winegar, N., 7, 11
Wolberg, 17
Wolf, A., 20
Wong, N., 149

Yalom, I. D., 21, 23, 51, 52, 54, 63-64,
    67, 87, 93, 117, 142-143, 148

Zaslav, M. R., 145

Subject Index

Access to care, 5, 8, 19, 22, 182
Addiction. *See* Substance abuse
    services
Addition, of group members, 77–78
Affect, and outcome, 172–173
Affordable Health Care Now Act, 9
Albany Social Phobia Protocol,
    154–155
Alcohol abuse, 66, 101, 102, 103, 104,
    106, 109, 123, 124, 125, 130. *See
    also* Substance abuse services
Alcoholics Anonymous, 107, 124, 125,
    126
American Association of Pastoral
    Care, 186
American Group Psychotherapy
    Association, *xi*, 183, 185–188
American Health Security Act, 9
American Medical Association, 13, 182
American Nurses' Association, 186
American Psychiatric Association, 6, 7,
    24, 31, 35, 177, 186
American Psychological Association,
    186
Appeal process, 41, 79
Assets, estimate of, 106. *See also*
    Resourses
Attendance, rules about, 78–79
Audiotaping, 74
Autonomy, of patient, 187

Axis I, 48, 104, 124
Axis II, 31, 48, 104, 124, 149, 152
Axis III, 31, 104, 124
Axis IV, 31–32, 104, 124
Axis V, 32, 104, 124

Barriers, to group participation, 84–85
Battered women, groups for, 77
Beck Depression Inventory, 154, 164
Beginning stage, 90
Behavioral approaches, 22, 50, 54, 66,
    71, 76, 94, 98, 113, 118–119, 148,
    153–156
Behavior rehearsal, 118
Behaviors, early-session, 111
Benefit packages, 8, 9–10, 30, 79
Bereavement groups, 77, 168–169
Billing procedures, 79
Bipolar Disorder, 177
Borderline personality disorder,
    149–152
Brief group psychotherapy, 15
    contemporary trends in, 21–28
    historical perspectives of, 16–21
    middle stage of. *See* Middle stage
    outcomes of. *See* Outcomes
    overview of pragmatics of, 29–41
Brief individual psychotherapy, 16–17,
    20, 21, 25–26, 46–47, 48–50,
    64–65, 66, 117

Brief psychotherapies, 11
rationale and goals of, 21–28
Burn out, 27

Canadian health care system, 9
Capitation, 14, 180–181, 182
Cardiac risk, groups for patients with, 77
Case history, of substance abuse, 101–102
Case management, 14
Case review, 168–169
Case reviewers, providers and, 180
Cathartic hypothesis, 172–173
Chafee S1770, 9
CHAMPUS, 9
Change, 26, 35, 65, 67, 68, 136
versus cure, 23–24
Characterological defenses, 53
Choice, 11–12, 13, 182
Chronically mentally ill patients, deinstitutionalization of, 4–5
Client. *See* Patient *entries*
Clinical practice guidelines, 176–178
Clinical setting, managed mental health care in, 3–15
Clinton plan, 8, 10, 12, 13, 181
Closing exercise/ritual, 134
Closing statement, 111, 112
Co-existing treatment, 79–81
Cognitive approaches, 50, 54, 66, 71, 76, 94, 113, 114, 115, 135, 148, 153–156, 173
Cohesion, 67, 92, 116, 175
Committee on Managed Care, APA, The, 31, 35
Communication workshop, 119
Community mental health movement, 17
Composition, of managed care group, 67–68, 72, 115–116
Computers, in future, 182
Concurrent review, 15, 34–39, 57, 115, 126. *See also* Tracking
Confidentiality, 72, 83, 109, 179, 187
Configurational analysis, 50
Construction, of managed care group, 58–68
Consumer Choice Health Security Act, 9
Consumers, 14
Contacts among group members, outside group session, 81–82, 109

Contract, group, modification of, 82
Cooper HR3222, 9
Core Conflict Relationship Theme (CCRT), 50
Costs, 5–6, 14, 22. *See also* Financing of plans
Co-therapy, 59, 95
Countertransferential blind spot, 129
Couples therapy, 80, 119–120. *See also* Marital therapy
Court mandated treatment, 31
Crises, 22, 53, 81, 119
Cure, change versus, 23–24
Current problems, 123

Deductibility, of premiums, 10
Deinstitutionalization, 4–5
Dependency, on leader, 110
Depression, 101, 102, 103, 104, 105, 123, 124, 168–169, 177
Development, group, stages of, 86–96
Diagnosis, 24, 31–32, 45, 48–50, 98, 104, 124, 126, 148, 154, 178
Diagnostic and Statistical Manual of Mental Disorders. See DSM *entries*
Differentiation, 88, 89
Difficult group members, 121–122
Dignity, of patient, 187
Dilution of transference, 128
Discharge planning, 39–40, 180
Discriminatory practices, 181, 182
Documenting. *See* Recording; Reporting
Downward drift, 51
Dropouts, 62, 77–78
Drug abuse, 66, 82, 101, 102, 103, 104, 105, 106, 107, 109, 117, 123, 125, 130. *See also* Substance abuse services
DSM-III-R, 6
DSM-IV, 31–32, 45, 48, 49–50, 98, 104, 124, 126, 148, 178
Dumping ground, 180
Dynamic group psychotherapy, long-term, 117

Early therapy stage, 92
Economics. *See* Costs
Educational experiences, in evaluation, 49
Ego psychology, 22
Eligibility Form, *xi*, 189–193

Emotional contagion, 62
Emotional intensity, of middle stage, 114–115
Employee assistance programs, 31
Employers, referral by, 31
Employment, 124
Encounter groups, 20, 21, 76, 117
Entry into group, 106–112
Ethical Guidelines, *xi*, 185–188
Ethical issues, 179–181
Evaluation. *See* Testing; Precertification review; Outcomes; Pre-group phase; and Retrospective review
Exclusion criteria, 51, 52–53, 55, 57, 109
Exercises, closing, 134

Facts and figures, 5–7
Family
    in evaluation, 49
    involvement of, 38, 106, 109, 147
Family therapy, 20, 21, 38, 80, 123
Fees, 79
Field theory, 20
Financing of plans, 8, 10. *See also* Costs
First group session, 106–112
Focal developmental conflict model, 91–93, 94
Focal group psychotherapy, 26–27
Follow-up, referral, 160, 162
Follow-up plan, 93, 127, 130, 133
Friendships, in evaluation, 49. *See also* Significant others
Functional impairments. *See* Impairment
Future, 181–183

Gatekeeper function, 11, 30, 160
Gestalt, 118
Global Assessment of Functioning (GAF), 32, 104, 124, 164
Goals, 22, 25, 26, 33–34, 37–38, 40, 76, 77, 105, 109, 111, 125, 143, 144
    establishment of, 65–67, 70–72
Go-arounds, 111–112
Grief, 77, 168–169. *See also* Mourning
Ground rules, 108–109
Group contract, modifications of, 82
Group development, stages of, 86–96
Group entry, preparation for. *See* Pre-group phase

Group leader. *See* Leaders
Group member(s)
    contacts and/or socialization among, outside of session, 81–82, 109
    difficult, 121–122
    loss and addition of, 77–78
    model treatment plan for specific, 101–112
    prospective. *See* Pre-group phase
Group note form, 164, 166
Group participation, barriers to, 84–85
Group psychotherapy
    brief. *See* Brief group psychotherapy
    emergence of, 5
    selection criteria for, 50–56
Group psychotherapy practice, guidelines of, 186–188
Groups
    inpatient. *See* Inpatient treatment
    managed care. *See* Managed care groups
    psychotherapy, 19
    self-help, 18
    typology of, 18–19
Group sessions. *See* Sessions
Group termination summary, 164, 167
Group therapists. *See* Therapists
Guidelines
    clinical practice, 176–178
    for ethics, 185–188
    of group psychotherapy practice, 186–188

Habit-control groups, 76
Harvard Community Health Plan, 174, 175
Health care
    impairments in, 124
    quality of, 13
Health care system, scope of problem of, 5–7
Health insurance. *See* Insurance
Health Maintenance Organizations (HMOs), 11, 13, 14, 91–93, 140
Health plans, prepaid, 22
Health Security Act, 8. *See also* Clinton plan
Health System Reform Proposal For Action, 13
Heterogeneity, 67–68, 149
Holding environment, 151
Homework, 26–27, 119

Homogeneity, 26, 55, 67–68, 91, 107,
146, 149
Hospitalization, 80–81, 109, 180. *See
also* Inpatient treatment
Hospitalized patient, with medical
illness, 146–148

Illegal aliens, 9
Impairment
individual, 51, 97–98, 105, 124–125,
141–142
severity of, 36, 104
Implications, for practitioners, 8,
11–12
Inclusion criteria, 50–56, 57, 109
Indian Health Service, 9
Individual level
for interventions, 119, 120
for tracking progress, 122–126, 168
Individual progress note form, 164, 165
Individual psychological impairment.
See Impairment
Individual therapy, 32, 64–65, 80
brief. *See* Brief individual
psychotherapy
Individuation, 89
Initial evaluation. *See* Precertification
review
Initial stage, 97–112
Initial treatment plan, review of,
97–101, 104–106
Inpatient psychiatric service, 140–146
Inpatient treatment, 35–39, 54, 76,
139–156. *See also* Hospitalization
to outpatient, 40
Insurance, health, 5, 13
Interactional variety, 68
Interim summary, 125–126
Interpersonal aspects, 32–33, 47, 48–50,
53, 55, 60, 87–89, 93–94, 142–143
Interpersonal closeness and distance, 88
Interpersonal content thematic evalua-
tion, 50
Interpersonal level, for interventions,
119–120
Interpersonal relationships. *See*
Relationships
Interpersonal status issues, 88
Interventions, 98–99, 105–106,
119–120, 122, 125

Intimacy, in relationships, 89
Involuntary referral, 31

Judgment day, 134

Language of managed care, 14–15
Lateness, 79
Late therapy stage, 92
Leaders
benefits to, 27–28
in middle stage, 115–122
and outcomes, 173–174
practical concerns for, 45–57
role and activity of, 58–65, 73–74
testing of, 110
Legal issues, 12, 13
Life-stage developmental perspective, 50
Liking group therapy, 40, 145
Limiting factors, 100
Long-term group, termination in, 132
Losses
adaptation to, 90–91, 168–169, 172, 173
of group members, 77–78. *See also*
Dropouts
termination, 128

Maintenance group therapy, 130–131
Malpractice, 8, 12
Managed care
initial stage of, 97–112
referral system of, 30
retrospective review in, 40–41
as term, 4
Managed care group members. *See*
Group members
Managed care groups, 19
composition of, 67–68, 72
construction of, 58–68
goals of. *See* Goals
management of issues prior to, 56–57
purpose of, 70–72
recording and reporting on, 159–169
size of, 59, 62, 78. *See also* Dropouts
structured, 153–156
termination of. *See* Termination
time factors in. *See* Time factors
with unique patient populations,
139–156
Managed care setting, stages of group
development in, 86–96

Managed competition, 7–8
Managed mental health care
  brief group therapy in. *See* Brief
    group psychotherapy
  general principles of, 3–15
  vocabulary of, 14–15
Managed Mental Health Care firm
  (MMHC), 11–12
Management of issues, prior to man-
  aged care group, 56–57
Marital therapy, 21, 119–120. *See also*
  Couples therapy
Matching fund, 10
McDermott HR1200, 9
Medicaid, 9, 10, 13
Medical illness, 36, 146–148
Medical savings accounts, 9
Medicare, 9, 10
Medication, 38–39, 80, 105, 106,
  124–126, 131, 145, 175, 179–180
Mental health care
  costs of, 5–6
  managed. *See* Managed mental
    health care
  reform of. *See* Reform
Mental status examination, 34, 36–37,
  103
Michel HR3080, 9
Middle stage, 90–91, 92, 113–126
  emotional intensity of, 114–115
Model setting participant, 63–64
Money matters, ethics in, 179
Monitoring, 14
Monitoring indicators, 173
Mood-related issues, 124–125
Mourning, 77, 91, 168–169. *See also*
  Grief
Mutuality, 89

National Advisory Mental Health
  Council, 181
National Data Bank, 12
National Federation of Societies for
  Clinical Social Work, 186
National Health Board, 8, 10
National Registry of Certified Group
  Psychotherapists, *xi*, 184, 189–193
Natural groups, 49
Nickles S1743, 9
Nonverbal communications, 111

Note taking, 161, 164, 165, 166, 168
Nursing, and ethics, 186

Object relations, 47, 53, 149, 150, 172
Observers, 74–75
One-stop shopping, in future, 182
Orientation. *See* Pre-group phase
Outcomes, 22, 99, 170–175
Outpatient treatment, 105, 106, 139
  inpatient to, 40

Party, termination, 133–134
Pastoral counselors, and ethics, 186
Patient, responsibility to, 186–188
Patient Impairment Profile (PIP), 98,
  100, 104
Patient populations, unique, 139–156
Patient Protection Act, 182
Payors, 14
Peer pressure, group, 116
Peers, in evaluation, 49
Personality disorders, groups for
  patients with, 148–152
Physical arrangement, of therapy room,
  75, 107–108
Physical illness. *See* Medical illness
Physicians. *See* Practitioners
Plan. *See* Follow-up plan; Treatment
  plan
Plan structure, 8–9, 30
Point of service (POS), 15
Practitioners. *See also* Providers
  implications of plans for, 8, 11–12
  primary, 11, 12, 30
Preaffiliation, 87–88
Precertification review, 14, 30–34, 39,
  57, 79, 159, 160
Precipitating circumstances, versus
  predisposing, 22
Preferred Health Care Ltd., 31
Preferred Provider Organizations, 11
Preferred providers, 15
Pre-group phase, 45–48, 69–85, 107,
  175
Pre-group preparation checklist, 71
Pre-group screening and diagnostic
  issues, 48–50
Prepaid health plans, 22
Preparation. *See* Pre-group phase
Presenting problems, 100, 104

Price controls, 13
Primary care, 11, 12, 30, 177
Privacy, 179, 187. *See also* Confidentiality
Private practice, 13
Problem-driven plan, 99
Problem patients, 121–122
Process review. *See* Concurrent review
Professional standards, 188
Progress
    tracking of, 122–126. *See also* Concurrent review
    versus regression, 35–36
Providers, *x*, 14. *See also* Leaders
    and case reviewers, 180
    preferred, 15
    role and activity of, 58–65, 73–74
Psychiatrists
    and ethics, 186
    future roles of, 182
Psychoanalytic approach, 20, 73, 94, 118, 142, 172
Psychodrama, 20
Psychodynamic aspects, 47, 52–53, 54, 87–90, 94, 113, 140–142, 173, 182–183
Psychological biopsy, 143
Psychological impairment. *See* Impairment
Psychological mindedness, 172
Psychologists, clinical, and ethics, 186
Purpose, of group, 70–72

Quality of health care, 13
Questions and answers, 83–84, 111

Recording, 159–164, 165, 166, 167
Referral follow-up form, 160, 163
Referral form, 160, 162
Referral system, managed care, 30, 79, 159, 160, 180
Reform
    implications of, for group therapists, 183–184
    plans for, 7–14
Regression, progress versus, 35–36
Relationships. *See also* Object relations; Significant others
    impairment of, 124
    intimacy in, 89
    sexual, in evaluation, 49
    therapeutic, 24–25
    trust in, 109

Relaxation, 146
Reporting, 159, 164, 168–169
Resistance, 84
Resources, of patient, 100. *See also* Assets
Responsibility, to patient/client, 186–188
Retrospective review, 15, 40–41, 79
Review
    concurrent. *See* Concurrent review
    of initial treatment plan, 97–101, 104–106
    precertification. *See* Precertification review
    retrospective, 15, 40–41, 79
Reviewer, case, provider and, 180
Rights, of patient, 187
Risk pools, 9
Rituals, closing, 134
Role-playing, 118
Room. *See* Therapy room
Route, of referral, 31
Rules, about attendance, 78–79

Safeguards, 187–188
Screening, pre-group, 48–50, 92
Selection criteria, for group psychotherapy, 50–56, 57
Self-disclosure
    by group members, 110
    by leader, 60
Self-help groups, 18, 107
Self-referral, 31
Sensitivity groups, 20, 76
Session(s)
    contacts and/or socialization among members outside of, 81–82
    first, 106–112
    last, 133–135
    length of, 76
    observers, audiotaping, or videotaping of, 74–75
Setting
    clinical, 3–15
    hospital, 139, 140–146
Severity of impairment, 36, 104
Sexual relationships, in evaluation, 49
Short-term anxiety provoking psychotherapy (STAPP), 46–47
Short-term therapy. *See* Brief *entries*
Significant others. *See also* Friendships; Peers; Relationships
    involvement of, 38

Single-payer system, 9
Sin taxes, 10
Size, group, 59, 62, 78. *See also* Dropouts
Slips, 109
Smoking cessation, 76
Socialization, among group members, outside of session, 81–82, 109
Social phobias, 154–155
Social workers, clinical, and ethics, 186
Specialists, 13
Splitting, 80
SSDI, 6
SSI, 6
Stages of group development, 86–96
Standardization, 176–178
Standards, professional, 188
Starting the group, 92
Stress reduction, 146
Structural Analysis of Social Behavior (SASB), 50, 164
Structure, plan, 8–9, 30
Structured managed care group models, 153–156, 172
Subcontracting, 150–151
Subsidization plans, 9, 10
Substance abuse services, 10, 12, 28, 83
  costs of, 5
  discharge planning in, 39–40
  family therapy in, 38
  goals of, 66
  leaders in, 116–117
  middle stage in, 123–125
  outside contacts among patients utilizing, 81–82
  termination in, 129–130
  treatment plan in, 101–112
Symptoms. *See* Impairments
Systems approaches, 25, 94, 142, 143–144

Target elements, in treatment plan, 102–104
Target goals. *See* Goals
Tax credits, 9
Taxes. *See also* Deductibility
  sin, 10
Technical eclecticism, in middle stage, 117–120
Technical expert, 63–64
Technique, in hospitals, 139
Technology transfer, 175

Termination, 88, 90–91, 92–93, 95, 127–136. *See also* Dropouts
  evolution of practices involving, 130–136
  leaders and, 61
Testing, 50. *See also* Mental status examination
  of leader, 110
"T"-groups, 20
Therapeutic mosaics, 117
Therapeutic relationship, 24–25
Therapies. *See specific therapies*; Treatment *entries*
Therapists, implications of reform for, 183–184
Therapy room, physical arrangement of, 75, 107–108
Time factors, 24, 25, 51, 76–77, 113–114, 174
Time-limited therapy. *See* Brief *entries*
Timing, of referral, 31
Tracking, progress, 122–126. *See also* Concurrent review
Transactional Analysis, 118
Transference, dilution of, 128
Transfer of learning, 23, 83, 118–119, 135
Treatment. *See also* Therapeutic *entries*
  co-existing, 79–81
Treatment plan
  components of, 37–38
  initial, 97–101, 104–106
  for specific managed care group member, 101–112
Trust, 90, 109
12-step programs, 39, 65, 107, 125

Universal coverage, 9, 13

Ventriloquist phenomenon, 116
Veterans Administration, 9
Videotaping, 74, 75
Vocabulary, 14–15
Voluntary referral, 31
Vouchers, 9

Weight loss groups, 76
Whole-group level
  for interventions, 119–120
  for tracking progress, 122–126
Workshops, 91–92, 119
World War II, 16, 20